EDWARD D. ANDREWS

MOSAIC AUTHORSHIP CONTROVERSY

Who Really Wrote the First Five Books of the Bible?

MOSAIC AUTHORSHIP CONTROVERSY

Who Really Wrote the First Five Books of the Bible?

Edward D. Andrews

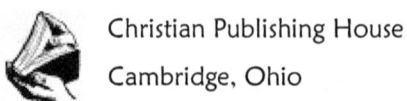

Christian Publishing House
Cambridge, Ohio

Copyright © 2019 Christian Publishing House

All rights reserved. Except for brief quotations in articles, other publications, book reviews, and blogs, no part of this book may be reproduced in any manner without prior written permission from the publishers. For information, write, support@christianpublishers.org

Unless otherwise indicated, Scripture quotations are from the Updated American Standard Version of the Holy Scriptures, 2019 edition (UASV).

MOSAIC AUTHORSHIP CONTROVERSY: Who Really Wrote the First Five Books of the Bible?

Authored by Edward D. Andrews

ISBN-13: **978-1-949586-79-4**

ISBN-10: **1-949586-79-0**

לכישפטם שפתי ויער להכסוון וקדותו פראיר עו   וילש ירטוק בישחק לי   בשרי אשר   הארץ
בראות ברע וזחבטן אל יעל לוא נוכל   אליוגר על יבוך וטוך על נגבייוק במלעוך   לוא אל אווך
בשר חדבר אשר לוא וכלות אל את על טוא א   נשוקף וסתתר ויקלסו בעוך רב וחוא   קל בל
ונווד בחוך וון אל אנ כשבטו כל אנוון וטוטו   לפוי בבוך ושוקף וצבור עפר ר. וערחר   ומרפפ
ואשפך כל רשע עפר אשר שפרי את פעותו   בשור על פרישך והכוואוף אשר יבו יא   יוסד וחוי
נפע למו נוא הוא אשר אף טחור שטוך פרא   טבערו וושפיוך ובל קצ ושחזקו אלוהוף   ע ברחוק
בשרי אשר לוא נוא אחד עטוחוך   לא כופת
חרישיוך לפח תבוטר ביארוף וחרוש בבלי   ובעך רב וקופוך לתעשך ובאפת ופחר   יאוך אשר
רשע עריץ פעו   נשרו על כות אבשר   ונתע טרוק וחרשיוך באון אוומטוך   תוך ופחחך
ואעשו אעשך אשך נשע בטוטות בדרך חיש   כהך או חלף דיח ועטר וישך וזח טוף   ברף נשר
דלוא שרוחד על איש וכוב   אשר פאח א   שי חנטראוך   לאלוחד   ף וויע x
התירוך בתיך של   ך ותעש ארץ ביאו   אשר ביעך בזה אשף   א עבורו איש x   ה אשר
ברמש למשליך ך ושחך וורקוחט   בלפור רעכו פרשל   א אחד וז קבלי   ובר x
וסעוך   לוודבר על בכ ו   ית בוח לאלוחו   שחית את זט
                       יפה איש   x טעוך   שטעוך

The Mosaic Authorship Controversy 6

Differences in Language and Style 39

Internal and External Evidence for Moses Authorship .. 47

Archaeology and the Bible 63

Concluding Thoughts 72

Genesis 10:5, 20, and 31 Indicate That There Were Many Languages, while 11:1 Says "One Language." Why? 85

The Old Testament Text 89

When Did the Hebrew Language Begin to Fade In Use?
.... 136

The Mosaic Authorship Controversy

It was in the latter half of the nineteenth century that higher criticism began to be taken seriously. These critics rejected Moses as the writer of the Pentateuch, arguing instead that the accounts in Genesis, Exodus, Leviticus, Numbers, and Deuteronomy were based on four other sources [writers] written between the 10th and the 6th centuries B.C.E. To differentiate these sources one from the other, they are simply known as the "J," "E," "D," and "P" sources. The letters are the initial to the name of these alleged sources, also known as the Documentary Hypothesis.

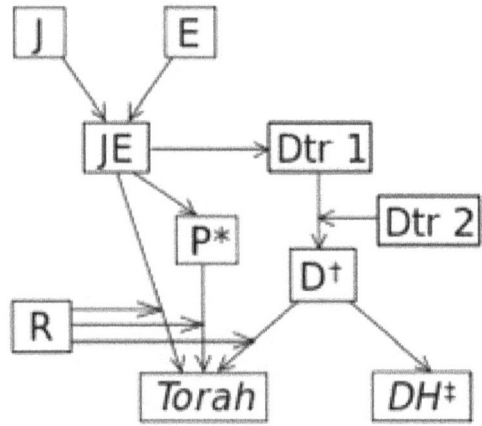

Diagram of the Documentary Hypothesis.
*   * includes most of Leviticus
*   † includes most of Deuteronomy
*   ‡ "Deuteronomic history": Joshua, Judges, 1 & 2 Samuel, 1 & 2 Kings – Wikipedia

Source Criticism, a sub-discipline of Higher Criticism, is an attempt by liberal Bible scholars to discover the original sources that the Bible writer(s) [not Moses] used to pen these five books. It should be noted that most scholars who engage in higher criticism start with liberal presuppositions. Dr. Gleason L. Archer, Jr., identifies many flaws in the reasoning of those who support the Documentary Hypothesis; however, this one flaw being quoted herein is indeed the most grievous and lays the foundation for other irrational reasoning in their thinking. Identifying their problem, Archer writes, "The Wellhausen school started with the pure assumption (which they have hardly bothered to demonstrate) that Israel's religion was of merely human origin like any other and that it was to be explained as a mere product of evolution."[1] In other words, Wellhausen and those who followed him begin with the presupposition that God's Word is *not* that at all, the Word of God, but is the word of mere man, and then they reason **into** the Scripture not **out of** the Scriptures based on that premise. As to the effect, this has on God's Word and those who hold it as such; it is comparable to having a natural disaster wash the foundation right out from under our home.

Liberal Christianity says that Moses did not pen every word from Genesis through Deuteronomy. They conclude that this is nothing more than a tradition that originated in the times that the Jews returned from their exile in Babylon in 537 B.C.E. and the destruction of Jerusalem in 70 C.E. These source critics reason that there was and is a misunderstanding of Deuteronomy 31:9, which says that Moses "[wrote] this law, and delivered it unto the priests the sons of Levi, that bare the ark of the covenant of Jehovah, and unto all the elders of Israel." They argue that

---

[1] 1. Gleason L. Archer, A Survey of Old Testament Introduction (Moody Publishers, Chicago, 2007), 98.

Deuteronomy only implies that Moses wrote the laws of Deuteronomy chapters 12–28; moreover, this was extended into a tradition that encompassed the belief that the entire Pentateuch was *not* written by Moses.

In addition, these source critics put forth that the language of Deuteronomy chapters 12–18, as well as the historical and theological context, places the writing and completion of these five books centuries after Moses died. According to these critics, this alleged tradition of Moses being the author of the first five books of our Bible was completely accepted as fact by the time Jesus Christ arrived on the scene in the first-century C.E. These critics further argue that Jesus, the Son of God, was also duped by this tradition and simply perpetuated it when he referred to "the book of Moses" (Mark 12:26), which to the Jews at that time counted Genesis, Exodus, Leviticus, Numbers, and Deuteronomy as a book by Moses. In addition, at John 17:23, Jesus spoke of "the law of Moses," which he and all other Jews had long held to be the Pentateuch. Thus, for the critic, Jesus simply handed this misunderstood tradition off to first-century Christianity.

We have read much in previous chapters thus far about these critical scholars, but it will not hurt to review, before delving into discrediting their hypothesis. How has such extreme thinking as this Documentary Hypothesis come down to us, going from being a hypothesis to being accepted as *law* in secular universities and most seminaries? What is the relationship between a hypothesis, theory, and law? In the physical sciences, there are several steps before a description of a phenomenon becomes law.

(1) **Observation:** "I noticed that objects fall to the earth."

(2) **Hypothesis:** "I think something must be pulling these objects to the earth. Let me call it gravity."

(3) **Experimentation:** "Let me put this to the test by releasing different objects from that cliff. Umm, it seems that everything I let go falls. My hypothesis seems to be right."

(4) **Theory:** "I have noticed that every time I release an object, and wherever I do it, over the sidewalk, from the 32nd floor of that office building and even from the cruise ship—they fall to the earth as if pulled by something. It happens often enough to be called a theory."

(5) **Law:** "Well, this has consistently been occurring over the years. It must be absolutely true and therefore a Law."

Where does the "Documentary Hypothesis" fit into this scheme? Wellhausen *et al.* made certain **Observations** and then produced a **Hypothesis** to explain what they saw. I would argue that is as far as they made it in following the formula for the scientific method.

The Forefathers of Source Criticisms

Abraham Ibn Ezra (1089–1164) Ibn Ezra was, by far, the most famous Bible scholar of medieval times. True enough, he may have questioned the idea that Moses wrote the entire Torah; however, he chose not to do this in an outward way; he chose to be more subtle in presenting such an idea. For Ibn Ezra, several verses seemed not to have come from Moses, but one verse stood out above the others. Deuteronomy 1:1 reads: "These are the words that Moses spoke to all of Israel beyond the Jordan." The east side of the Jordan would be "this" side with the west side being the "other side." (Numbers 35:14; Joshua 22:4) The point of his contention here is the fact that Moses was never on the other side of the Jordan, the west side, with the Israelite nation.

Therefore, the question begs to be asked, Why would Moses pen "beyond," a seeming reference to the west side? This will be answered soon enough.

Thomas Hobbes (1588–1679) writes, "It is therefore sufficiently evident that the five books of Moses were written after his time, though how long after it be not so manifest." Is Hobbes a friend or foe of Christianity? Like Francis Bacon before him, he deepened the crack in the acceptance of the Bible being a source of divine authority.[2]

Benedict Spinoza (1632–1677) writes, "It is thus clearer than the sun at noon the Pentateuch was not written by Moses but by someone who lived long after Moses." Spinoza lays the groundwork for higher criticism based on logical or reasonable deduction, believing that thought and actions should be governed by reason, deductive rationalism.[3] He writes that because "There are many passages in the Pentateuch which Moses could not have written, it follows that the belief that Moses was the author of the Pentateuch is ungrounded and irrational."[4] Moses was not the only Biblical author to lose his writership at the chopping block of Spinoza. "I pass on, then, to the prophetic books ... An examination of these assures me that the prophecies therein contained have been compiled from other books ... but are only such as were collected here and there, so that they are fragmentary." Daniel did not fare so well either; he is only credited with the last five chapters of his book. Spinoza presents the notion that the 39 books of the Hebrew Old

---

[2] Garrett, Don, *The Cambridge companion to Spinoza* (Cambridge: Cambridge University Press, 1996), 389.

[3] Richard Elliot Friedman, *Who Wrote The Bible* (San Francisco: Harper Collins, 1997), 21.

[4] R. H. M. Elwes, *A Theologico-political Treatise, and a Political Treatise* (New York, NY: Cosimo Classics, 2005), 126.

Testament were set down by none other than the Pharisees. Moreover, the prophets spoke not by God, being inspired, but of their own accord. As to the apostles, Spinoza wrote, "The mode of expression and discourse adopted by [them] in the Epistles show very clearly that the latter are not written by revelation and divine command, but merely by the natural powers and judgment of the authors." Did Matthew, Mark, Luke, and John, fare any better? Hardly! Spinoza states: "It is scarcely credible that God can have designated to narrate the life of Christ four times over, and to communicate it thus to mankind."

Spinoza had no respect for those he deemed fools because of their belief in miracles. He writes, "Anyone who seeks for the true causes of miracles and strives to understand natural phenomena as an intelligent being, and not gaze upon them like a fool, is set down and denounced as an impious heretic by those, whom the masses adore as the interpreters of nature and the gods. Such a person knows that, with the removal of ignorance, the wonder which forms their only available means for proving and preserving their authority would vanish also. . . . A miracle, whether a contravention to or beyond nature is a mere absurdity."[5] Such dogmatic disbelief in miracles is a contributing factor to Spinoza being the father of modern-day higher criticism.

Richard Simon (1638–1712). This French Catholic priest accepted Moses as the author for most of the Pentateuch, but he is the first to notice repetition with certain portions that would come to be known as doublets.

- two different creation stories

---

[5] Norman L. Geisler, *Inerrancy* (Grand Rapids, MI: Zondervan, 1980), 318.

- two stories of the Abrahamic covenant
- two stories where Abraham names his son, Isaac
- two stories where Abraham claims Sarah as his sister
- two stories of Jacob's journey to Haran
- two stories where God revealed himself to Jacob at Bethel
- two stories where God changes Jacob's name to Israel
- two stories of when Moses got water from a rock at Meribah

Jean Astruc (1684–1766) This French physician and professor of medicine would, by a rather naïve observation, get the Documentary Hypothesis underway. While Astruc never denied Mosaic writership, he had observed that there seemed to be two sources for Moses' penning the early chapters of Genesis: one that favored the title God (Elohim), and another that favored the personal name of God (Jehovah). This theory seemed to carry even more support by duplicate material, as Astruc viewed Genesis chapter one as one creation account and Genesis chapter two as another. It should be kept in mind that Astruc credited Moses as the writer, but was simply looking for what Moses may have drawn on in penning the Pentateuch.[6]

David Hume (1711–1776) was an eighteenth-century Scottish philosopher whose influence on the denial of divine authority, miracles, and prophecy has had a major impact that has reached down to the twenty-first century!

---

[6] Norman L. Geisler and William E. Nix, *A General Introduction to the Bible. Rev. and Expanded* (Chicago, IL: Moody Press, c.1986, 1996), 156.

Hume has three major pillars that hold up his refutation of divine authority. First, he writes, "A miracle is a violation of the laws of nature."[7] The laws of nature have been with man since his start. If a person falls from a high place, he will hit the ground. If a rock is dropped into the sea, it will sink. Each morning our sun comes over the horizon, and each night it goes down, and so on. Without a doubt, there are laws of nature that never fail to follow their purpose. Therefore, for Hume, there is nothing that would ever violate the laws of nature. This 'conclusive evidence,' Hume felt, "is as entire as any argument from experience" that there could never be miracles.

Hume's second pillar is based on his belief that humankind is gullible. Moreover, he reasons that the masses of 'religious persons' want to believe in miracles. In addition, there have been many who have lied about so-called miracles, which have been nothing but a sham. For his third pillar, Hume argues that miracles have occurred only in the time periods of ignorance; as the enlightenment of man grew the miraculous diminished. Hume reported, "Such prodigious events never happen in our days." Hume rejected the inspiration of Scripture on two grounds: (1) he denied the possibility of miracles and prophecy, and (2) he rejected the Bible's divine authority as a whole because, to him, it was based on perception or feeling, rather than upon fact, nor could it be proved by observation and experiment. Thus, for Hume, the result is that the Bible "contains nothing but sophistry and illusion."[8] As we can see, Hume's conclusion is obvious: Because the Bible is, in fact, not inspired, it could never be a true source of

---

[7] David Hume, *An Enquiry Concerning Human Understanding* (Boston, MA: Digireads.com, 2006), 65.

[8] Ibid., 90.

knowledge that it claims, and it is certainly not God's Word for humankind.

Johann Gottfried Eichhorn (1752–1827) took Jean Astruc's conjectures beyond Genesis to other books of the Pentateuch, arguing that the Pentateuch contained three primary sources that were distinct by vocabulary, style, and theological features. He also borrowed the phrase "higher criticism" from Presbyterian minister and scientist Joseph Priestly, and he was the first to name these alleged sources "E" (for Elohim) and "J" for Jehovah.[9]

Karl Heinrich Graf (1815–1869), aside from Julius Wellhausen, was the person we look to most for the modern documentary hypothesis. For Graf the "J" source was the earliest, composed in the ninth century B.C.E.;[10] the "E" source was written shortly thereafter. The author of Deuteronomy wrote shortly before Josiah's clearing away false worship in the seventh century B.C.E., and finally, the "P" source was written in the sixth century after the exile.

In 1878, the German Bible critic **Julius Wellhausen (1844–1918),** writing in *Prolegomena zur Geschichte Israels* (*Prolegomena to the History of Israel*), popularized the ideas of the above scholars that the first five books of the Bible, as well as Joshua, were written from the 9th century

---

[9] Norman L. Geisler and William E. Nix, *A General Introduction to the Bible. Rev. and Expanded* (Chicago, IL: Moody Press, c.1986, 1996), 157.

[10] B.C.E. means "before the Common Era," which is more accurate than B.C. ("before Christ"). C.E. denotes "Common Era," often called A.D., for anno Domini, meaning "in the year of our Lord."

into the 5th century B.C.E., over a millennium [1,000 years] after the events described.[11]

The capital letter "J" is used to represent an alleged writer. In this case, it stands for any place God's personal name, Jehovah, is used. It is argued that this author is perhaps a woman as it is the only one of their presented authors who is not a priest. (Harold Bloom, *The Book of "J"*) They date the portion set out to "J" to c.850 B.C.E. Some scholars place this author in the southern portion of the Promised Land, Judah.[12]

Another writer is put forth as "E," for it stands for the portion that has Jehovah's title Elohim, God. Most higher critics place this author c.750–700 B.C.E. Unlike "J," this author "E" is said to reside in the northern kingdom of Israel. As stated earlier, this author is reckoned a priest, with his lineage going back to Moses. It is also proffered that he bought this office. In addition, it is argued that an editor combined "J" and "E" after the destruction of Israel by the Assyrians but before the destruction of Jerusalem by the Babylonians, which they date to about 722 BC.E.[13]

These same critics hold out that the language and theological content of "D," Deuteronomy, is different from Genesis, Exodus, Leviticus, and Numbers. Thus they have another author. They argue that the priests living in the northern kingdom of Israel gathered "D" over several hundred years; however, it was not until much later that "D" was combined with the earlier works. It is also said that the "D" writer (source) was also behind Joshua,

---

[11] Ernest Nicholson, The Pentateuch in the Twentieth Century: The Legacy of Julius Wellhausen (New York: Oxford University Press, 1998), 36–47.

[12] Mark F. Rooker, *Leviticus: The New American Commentary* (Nashville: Broadman & Holman, 2001), 23.

[13] Ibid., 23.

Judges, 1 and 2 Samuel and 1 and 2 Kings (Dtr). It is suggested strongly that, in fact, this is the book found in the temple by Hilkiah, the high priest and given to King Josiah. (2 Kings 22:8) It is further put forth that J/E/D were fused together as one document in about 586 B.C.E.[14]

The source critics use the capital letter "P" for Priestly. This is because this portion of the Pentateuch usually relates to the priesthood. For instance, things like the sacrifices would be tagged as belonging to this author. Many scholars suggest that "P" was written before the destruction of Jerusalem, which they date at 586 B.C.E. Others put forth that it was written during the exile of seventy years, the Priest(s) composing this holy portion for the people who would return from exile, while others say it was written after the exile, about 450 B.C.E. These liberal scholars find no consensus on when this supposed author "P" wrote this portion of the first five books. The critics tell us that the final form of J/E/D/P was composed into one document about 400 B.C.E.[15]

The capital "R" represents the editor(s) who put it together and may have altered some portions to facilitate their social-circumstances of their day. The "R" comes from the German word *Redakteur* (Redactor), which is an editor or reviser of a work.

With all the focus on Wellhausen and the impetus he has given to the Documentary Hypothesis, one would conclude that he had made an enormous, critical investigation of the text, which, in essence, moved him to cosign with his predecessors. If that is your conclusion, you will have to regroup, for it was simply a feeling that something was not quite right that moved Wellhausen to accept a system of understanding without any evidence

---

[14] Ibid., 23.

[15] Ibid., 23–24.

whatsoever. In his book *Prolegomena to the History of Israel*, first published in 1878, Wellhausen helps his readers to appreciate just how he came about his expressed interest in the Documentary Hypothesis:

> In my early student days I was attracted by the stories of Saul and David, Ahab and Elijah; the discourses of Amos and Isaiah laid strong hold on me, and I read myself well into the prophetic and historical books of the Old Testament. Thanks to such aids as were accessible to me, I even considered that I understood them tolerably, but at the same time was troubled with a bad conscience, as if I were beginning with the roof instead of the foundation; for I had no thorough acquaintance with the Law, of which I was accustomed to be told that it was the basis and postulate of the whole literature. At last I took courage and made my way through Exodus, Leviticus, Numbers, and even through Knobel's Commentary to these books. But it was in vain that I looked for the light which was to be shed from this source on the historical and prophetical books. On the contrary, my enjoyment of the latter was marred by the Law; it did not bring them any nearer me, but intruded itself uneasily, like a ghost that makes a noise indeed, but is not visible and really effects nothing. Even where there were points of contact between it and them, differences also made themselves felt, and I found it impossible to give a candid decision in favour of the priority of the Law. Dimly I began to perceive that throughout there was between them all the difference that separates two wholly distinct worlds. Yet, so far from attaining clear conceptions, I only fell into deeper confusion,

which was worse confounded by the explanations of Ewald in the second volume of history of Israel. At last, in the course of a casual visit in Göttingen in the summer of 1867, I learned through Ritschl that Karl Heinrich Graf placed the law later than the Prophets, and, almost without knowing his reasons for the hypothesis, I was prepared to accept it; I readily acknowledged to myself the possibility of understanding Hebrew antiquity without the book of the Torah.[16]

Martin Noth (1902–1968) A liberal twentieth-century German scholar who specialized in the pre-Exilic history of the Jewish people. Noth presented what he called the "Deuteronomic Historian." He argued that the language and theological outlook of Joshua, Judges, 1 and 2 Samuel and 1 and 2 Kings was the same as the book of Deuteronomy. Noth believed this writer lived during the exile because of a reference from 2 Kings to the exile. Modern critics, however, believed this writer lived before the exile, with 2 Kings 25:27 being a later addition.

Frank M. Cross, Jr., Hebrew, and Biblical scholar' muddies the water even more with his proposition that there was not one Deuteronomistic history, but two. The first he proposed to be written during the reign of the Judean King Josiah to aid him in cleaning up the false worship going on within Judah. After the destruction of Jerusalem, Cross said the same writer or possibly another goes back to edit this work, to add in the destruction of Jerusalem and the exile to Babylon.

---

[16] Julius Wellhausen, Prolegomena to the History of Israel (1878), 3–4

Redaction Criticism

I briefly address the Redaction Theory here because of its relationship to the Documentary Hypothesis. As stated above in our alphabet soup of alleged authors ("J," "E," "D," "P," and "R"), a redactor is an editor or reviser of a work. Redaction Criticism is another form of Biblical criticism that intends to investigate the Scriptures and draw conclusions concerning their authorship, historicity, and time of writing. This form of criticism, as well as the others, has really done nothing more than tear down God's Word. R. E. Friedman, the Documentary Hypothesis' biggest advocate, asserts that the "J" document was composed between 922–722 B.C.E. in the southern kingdom of Judah, while the northern kingdom of Israel was composing the "E" document during these same years. Friedman contends that sometime thereafter a compiler of history put these two sources together, resulting in "J/E," with the compiler being known as "RJE." Friedman states that shortly thereafter, the priesthood in Jerusalem put out yet another document, known today as "P," this being another story to be added to the above "J/E." Going back to their authors for the first five books of the Bible, Friedman and these critics claim a redactor, or editor put the whole Pentateuch together using "D," "P," and the combination of "J/E." For them, this editor (Deuteronomist) used the written sources he had available to make his additions for dealing with the social conditions of his day. They claim this editor's express purpose was to alter Scripture to bring comfort and hope to those who were in exile in Babylon. Wellhausen's theories, with some adjustments, have spread like a contagious disease, until they have consumed the body of Christendom. However, the real question is, Do these higher critics have any serious evidence to overturn thousands of years of belief by three major religious groups (Jews, Christians, and Muslims) that the Pentateuch was written by Moses?

What these critics have are pebbles, each representing minute inferences and implications [circumstantial evidence at best] that they place on one side of a scale. These are weighed out against the conservative evidence of Moses' authorship of the Pentateuch. As unsuspecting readers work their way through the books and articles written by these critics, the scales seem to be tilted all to one side, as if there were no evidence for the other side. Thus, like a jury, many uninformed readers; conclude that there is no alternative but to accept the idea that there are multiple authors for the Pentateuch instead of Moses, who is traditionally held to be the sole author.

Just what impact has the Documentary Hypothesis had on academia? Let us allow R. Rendtorf, Professor Emeritus of the University of Heidelberg, to answer:

> Current international study of the Pentateuch presents at first glance a picture of complete unanimity. The overwhelming majority of scholars in almost all countries where scholarly study of Old Testament is pursued, take the documentary hypothesis as the virtually uncontested point of departure for their work; and their interest in the most precise understanding of the nature and theological purposes of the individual written sources seems undisturbed.[17]

Let us take a moment to look at many of these pebbles and see which side of the scale they are to be placed on. As stated at the outset, we will address the

---

[17] R. Rendtorff, "The Problem of the Process of Transmission in the Pentateuch," *JSOT* (1990): 101.

major arguments as a case against the whole. Some of these pebbles are major obstacles for honest-hearted Christians.

Arguments of Higher Critics for the Documentary Hypothesis

We will address four areas of argumentation from the higher critics: (1) the divine names, (2) discrepancies, (3) repetition, known as "doublets," and (4) differences in language and style. We will give at least one example of each and address at least one example under the evidence for Moses' writership.

Divine Names

The higher critics argue that every Bible verse that contains the Hebrew word for God, (*'Elohim'*), set off by itself has its own writer, designated by the capital "E" ("Elohist"). On the other hand, any verse that contains the Tetragrammaton, (Jehovah, Yahweh), God's personal name, is attributed to yet another writer, "J" ("Jawist"). (Cassuto, 18-21) Let us see how they explain this. The critics argue that "God" (*'Elohim'*) is restricted in use exclusively in the first chapter of Genesis (1:1–31) in relation to God's creation activity, and that starting in Genesis 2:4 through the end of the second chapter we find God's personal name.

R. E. Friedman speaks of a discovery by three men: "One was a minister, one was a physician, and one was a professor. The discovery that they made ultimately came down to the combination of two pieces of evidence: doublets and the names of God. They saw that there were apparently two versions each of a large number of Biblical stories: two accounts of the creation, two accounts each of several stories about the patriarchs Abraham and Jacob, and so on. Then, they noticed that, quite often, one of the two versions of a story would refer to God by one name and the other version would refer to God by a different name." (R. E. Friedman, 50)

Different settings, however, require different uses. This principle holds true throughout the whole of the entire Old Testament. Moses may choose to use ('*Elohim*') in a setting in which he wants to show a particular quality clearly, like power, creative activity, and so on. On the other hand, Moses may choose to use God's personal name (Jehovah, Yahweh) when the setting begs for that personal relationship with the Father and his children, the Israelites, or even more personable, a one-on-one conversation between Jehovah God and a faithful servant.

The Divine Names: The weakness of claiming multiple authors because of the different names used for God is quite evident when we look at just one small portion of the book of Genesis in the *American Standard Version* (1901). God is called "God Most High," "possessor (or maker) of heaven and earth," "O Lord Jehovah," "a God that seeth," "God Almighty," "God," "[the] God,"[18] and "the Judge of all the earth." (Genesis 14:18, 19; 15:2; 16:13; 17:1, 3; 18:25) It is difficult to believe that different authors wrote these verses. Moreover, let us look at Genesis 28:13, which says, "And, behold, Jehovah stood above it, and said, I am Jehovah, the God ["Elohim"] of Abraham thy father, and the God of Isaac: the land whereon thou liest, to thee will I give it, and to thy seed." Another scripture, Psalm 47:5, says, "God is gone up with a shout, Jehovah with the sound of a trumpet."[19] In

---

[18] The title '*Elo·him*' preceded by the definite article *ha*, giving the expression *ha·'Elo·him*'.

[19] See also Psalm 46:11; 48:1, 8.

applying their documentary analysis, we would have to accept the idea that two authors worked together on each of these two verses.

Many conservative scholars have come to realize that in a narrative format one will often find a ruler being referred to not only by name but also by a title, such as "king." M. H. Segal observes: "Just as those interchanges of human proper names and their respective appellative common nouns cannot by any stretch of the imagination be ascribed to a change of author or source of document, so also the corresponding interchanges of the divine names in the Pentateuch must not be attributed to such a literary cause."[20] If one were to look up "Adolf Hitler" using Academic American Encyclopedia, within three paragraphs he will find the terms "Führer," "Adolf Hitler," and simply "Hitler." Who is so bold as to suggest that there are three different authors for these three paragraphs?

Dr. John J. Davis[21] helps us to appreciate that there is "no other religious document from the ancient Near East [that] was compiled in such a manner; a documentary analysis of the Gilgameš Epic or Enūma Eliš would be complete folly. The author of Genesis may have selected divine names on the basis of theological emphasis rather than dogmatic preference. Many divine names were probably interchangeable; Baal and Hadad were used

---

[20] See also Psalm 46:11; 48:1, 8.

[21] John J. Davis, *Paradise to Prison: Studies in Genesis* (Salem: Sheffield, 1975), 22–23.

interchangeably in the Hadad Tablet from Ugarit,[22] and similar examples could be cited from Egyptian texts."[23]

In fact, we now know that there were many deities in the ancient Near East that had multiple names. As stated above with the Babylonian Creation account, the Enuma Elish, the god Marduk (Merodach), chief deity of Babylon, also had some 50 different names.[24] It would not even be thinkable to apply any of the Documentary Hypothesis analysis to any of these works. Why? Not only because we can see that ancient writers are no different from modern writers and are able to use different names and titles interchangeably within their work, but they were written on stone, so to speak. If one has one clay tablet that has both a personal name and two different titles for the same king, it would be difficult to argue that there were two or three different authors for the one tablet. Bible scholar Mark F. Rooker has the following to say about the use of Elohim and Yahweh in the Old Testament:

> Moreover, it is clear that throughout the Old Testament that the occurrence of the names of God as Elohim or Yahweh is to be attributed to contextual and semantic issues, not the existence of sources. This conclusion is borne out by the fact that the names consistently occur in predictable genre. In the legal and prophetic texts the name Yahweh always appears, while in wisdom literature the name for God is invariably Elohim. In narrative literature, which includes

---

[22] G. R. Driver, *Canaanite Myths and Legends* (New York: T. & T. Clark, 1971), 70-72.

[23] For example, see the "Stele of Ikhernofret" in James B. Pritchard, ed., *Ancient Near Eastern Texts*, 2nd ed. Princeton: Princeton University Press, 1955, pp. 329–30.

[24] K. A. Kitchen, *On the Reliability of the Old Testament* (Grand Rapids: Eerdmans, 2003), 424–5.

much of the Pentateuch, both Yahweh and Elohim are used.[25] Yet consistently the names do not indicate different sources but were chosen by design. The name Elohim was used in passages to express the abstract idea of Deity as evident in God's role as Creator of the universe and the Ruler of nature. Yahweh, on the other hand, is the special covenant name of God who has entered into a relationship with the Israelites since the name reflects God's ethical character. (Cassuto, 31) Given the understanding of the meaning of these names for God, it is no wonder that the source which contains the name Yahweh would appear to reflect a different theology from a selected group of texts which contained the name Elohim."[26]

Let us, on a small scale, do our own analysis of the divine names in the first two chapters of Genesis. The Hebrew word (*'elohim*') is most often agreed upon to be from a root meaning "be strong," "mighty," or "power."[27] It should be said too that by far, most Hebrew scholars recognize the plural form (*im*) of this title *'elo·him*' to be used as a plural of "majesty," "greatness," or "excellence." The Hebrew word (*'elo·him*') is used for the Creator 35 times from Genesis 1:1 to 2:4a. Exactly what is the context of this use? It is used in a setting that deals with God's power, his greatness, his excellence, his creation activity, all of which seems appropriate, does it not?

---

[25] Similarly, Livingston has pointed out that the cognate West Semitic divine names il and ya(w) appear to be interchangeable in the Eblaite tablets. (*The Pentateuch in Its Cultural Environment*, 224.)

[26] Mark F. Rooker, *Leviticus: The New American Commentary* (Nashville: Broadman & Holman, 2001), 26–27.

[27] Ibid., 27.

Moving on to Genesis 2:4b–25, we find God now being referred to by his personal name, the Tetragrammaton (YHWH, JHVH), which is translated "Jehovah" (KJV, ASV, NW, NEB, etc.) or "Yahweh" (AT, NAB, JB, HCSB, etc.). It is found in verses 4b–25 eleven times; however, it comes before his title ('*elohim*').[28] Why the switch, and what is the context of this use? This personal name of God is used in a setting that deals with his personal relationship with man and woman. This is not a second creation account; it is a more detailed account of the creation of man, which was only briefly mentioned in chapter one in passing, as each feature of creation was ticked off. In chapter two, the Creator becomes a person as he speaks to his intelligent creation, giving them the prospect of a perfect eternal life in a paradise garden, which is to be cultivated earth wide, to be filled with perfect offspring. Therefore, we see a personal interchange between God and man as He lays out His plans to Adam, which seems very appropriate, does it not when switching from using a title in chapter one to using a personal name in chapter two? In chapter two, we have the coupling of the personal name "Jehovah" with the title "God," to show that we are still talking about this 'great,' 'majestic,' 'all powerful' Creator, but personalized as he introduces himself to his new earthly creation.

Thus, there is no reason to assume that we are talking about two different writers. No, it is two different settings in which a skilled writer would make the transition just as Moses did. It would be no different than if a modern-day news commentator was giving as a report about the United States President visiting Russia to meet with Dmitry Anatolyevich Medvedev, in which he used the title President predominately. The following week the same news commentator may be covering the President visiting

---

[28] "Jehovah God." Heb., Yehwah´ 'Elohim´.

a hospital with injured children who had survived a tornado and refer to the President as President Obama. It isn't difficult to see that one is an official setting where the President needs to be portrayed as powerful, while in the other setting; he needs to be portrayed as personable. The same principles used herein apply to the rest of the Pentateuch and the Old Testament as a whole.

Discrepancies

Discrepancies, or should I say "perceived" discrepancies, are the critic's favorite pebble. These perceived discrepancies set off an alarm for the critic, and then he rushes off with his pebble like a child to add it to the multiple-authors side of the scale. To differentiate between the supposed different sources texts, I will lay them out as follows:

> **("J")** will be used to represent an alleged writer. In this case, it stands for any place God's name Jehovah is used.
>
> **("E")** will be for the portion that has Jehovah's title, *Elohim,* God.
>
> **("P")** will be for the portion of priestly activities.
>
> **("D")** Deuteronomy is different from Genesis, Exodus, Leviticus, and Numbers. Thus, it has another author.
>
> **("RJE")** will represent the compiler who put "J" and "E" together.
>
> **("R")** will represent the editor(s), who put it all together and may have altered some portions to express their social circumstances of their day.
>
> **("U")** will represent the alleged "unknown independent texts."

"Narrative Discrepancy" (Genesis 12:1, ASV) Now Jehovah said unto Abram, Get thee out of thy country, and from thy kindred, and from thy father's house, unto the land that I will show thee: ("J") (after Terah, Abram's father, died, Abram is commanded to leave Haran)

> **(Genesis 11:26, ESV)** When Terah had lived 70 years, he fathered Abram, Nahor, and Haran ("U"). (When Terah was 70, Abram was born.)
>
> **(Genesis 11:32, ESV)** The days of Terah were 205 years ("U"): and Terah died in Haran ("R"). (Terah died at the age of 205, which would make Abraham 135 when he left Ur.)
>
> **(Genesis 12:4, ASV)** So Abram went, as Jehovah had spoken unto him; and Lot went with him ("J"): and Abram was seventy and five years old when he departed out ("P") of Haran ("R"). (12:4 has Abram being only 75 when he leaves Haran.)

Discrepancy: According to 11:32, Terah died at the age of 205; hence, Abram must have been 135 when he was called to leave Haran. However, 12:4 says that he was only 75 when he left Haran. The Source Critic informs us that this seeming contradiction is resolved if Genesis chapter 12 is of a different source from the genealogy of Genesis chapter 11.

The above need not be a contradiction at all. True enough, it was at the age of 70 that Terah began having children (Genesis 11:26), but does Abraham have to be the firstborn child simply because he is listed first? Consider, what weight do the names Nahor and Haran play in the Bible account? Now consider, what about the name

Abraham? He is considered the father and founder of three of the greatest religions on this planet: Judaism, Christianity, and Islam. He is the third most prominent person named in God's Word. This practice, that of placing the most prominent son first in a list of sons even though they are not the firstborn is followed elsewhere in God's Word with other prominent men of great faith, for example, Shem and Isaac. (Genesis 5:32; 11:10; 1 Chronicles 1:28) Therefore, let us keep it simple. Genesis 11:26 does not say that Abram was the firstborn; it simply says that Terah began fathering children, and then it goes on to list his three sons, listing the most prominent one first. Thus, it is obvious that Terah fathered Abram at the age of 130. (Genesis 11:26, 32; 12:4) In addition, it is true that Sarah was Abram's half-sister, not by the same mother, but by having Terah as the same father. (Genesis 20:12) Therefore, in all likelihood, it is Haran who is the firstborn of Terah, whose daughter was old enough to marry Nahor, another of Terah's three sons. – Genesis 11:29.

"Narrative Discrepancy" (Genesis 37:25–28, 36; 38:1; 39:1, YLT)

> **(Genesis 37:25–28, YLT)** And they sit down to eat bread ("E"), and they lift up their eyes, and look, and lo, a company of Ishmaelites coming from Gilead, and their camels bearing spices, and balm, and myrrh, going to take [them] down to Egypt. 26 And Judah saith unto his brethren, 'What gain when we slay our brother, and have concealed his blood? 27 Come, and we sell him to the Ishmaelites, and our hands are not on him, for he [is] our brother—our flesh;' and his brethren hearken ("J"). 28 And Midianite merchantmen pass by and they

draw out and bring up Joseph out of the pit ("E"), and sold him to the Ishmaelites for twenty shekels of silver. They took Joseph to Egypt ("J"). (Genesis 37:36) And the Medanites have sold him unto Egypt, to Potiphar, a eunuch of Pharaoh, head of the executioners ("E"). (Genesis 38:1) And it cometh to pass, at that time, that Judah goeth down from his brethren, and turneth aside unto a man, an Adullamite, whose name [is] Hirah ("J"). (Genesis 39:1) And Joseph hath been brought down to Egypt, and Potiphar, a eunuch of Pharaoh, head of the executioners, an Egyptian man, buyeth him out of the hands of the Ishmaelites who have brought him thither ("J").

Discrepancy: In Genesis 37:25 the Ishmaelites are passing by at the opportune time mentioned in verses 26 and 27, with Judah suggesting that instead of killing Joseph they sell him to the Ishmaelites. Yet, verse 28 switches in midstride to the Midianites, as they drew Joseph from the pit, selling him to the Ishmaelites. In verse 36, the Medanites (likely a scribal error; almost every translation has Midianites, so we will accept that as so) are selling Joseph to Potiphar in Egypt. Yet, the discrepancy pushes the envelope even further, for Genesis 39:1 says, it was the Ishmaelites who delivered and sold Joseph to Potiphar in Egypt. Was Joseph sold to Ishmaelites or to Midianites? In addition, who delivered and sold Joseph to Potiphar in Egypt? It seems that the higher critics are bent on using ambiguous passages (ambiguous at first glance to the casual reader) to facilitate their Documentary Hypothesis. You might say that these discrepancies are fuel for the engine that drives their Documentary Hypothesis locomotive. E. A. Speiser writes:

The narrative is broken up into two originally independent versions. One of these (J) used the name Israel, featured Judah as Joseph's protector, and identified the Ishmaelites as the traders who bought Joseph from his brothers. The other (E) spoke of Jacob as the father and named Reuben as Joseph's friend; the slave traders in that version were Midianites who discovered Joseph by accident and sold him in Egypt to Potiphar.[29]

For Speiser, it is time to slice up the text and divide it up between our alleged "J"-Text and "E"-Text writers. It is also hypothesized that our "R"-Redactor edits the two and slips in some additional information as well, suggesting that the Midianites are the ones who were actually passing by, selling Joseph later to the Ishmaelites. Thus, it would be the Ishmaelites, who would deliver and sell Joseph to Potiphar in Egypt. Yes, at first glimpse, this would appear to make it all well, but we still have a problem: Genesis 37:36 states that it was the Midianites, who sold Joseph to Potiphar in Egypt.

Actually, when one looks below the surface reading, there is no discrepancy here at all. Ishmael (son of Hagar and Abraham) and Midian (son of Keturah and Abraham) were half-brothers. It is highly likely that there was intermarriage between the descendants of these two, allowing for interchangeable use of the expression "Ishmaelites" and "Midianites." (Genesis 25:1–4; 37:25–28; 39:1) We see this in the days of Judge Gideon when Israel was being attacked, with both terms "Ishmaelites" and "Midianites" being used to describe the attackers. (Judges 8:24; 7:25; 8:22, 26) Alternatively, even still we

---

[29] E. A. Speiser, *Genesis*, Anchor Bible (Garden City, N.Y.: Doubleday, 1964), 293–4.

could have an Ishmaelite caravan encompassing Midianite merchants that were passing by, with the Midianites brokering the deal and delivering Joseph from the pit to the Ishmaelite caravan, where Joseph would be under the Ishmaelites' custody even if he was being *detained* by the Midianites. Once they arrived at Potiphar's place in Egypt, it would be the Midianites to broker the deal with Potiphar. Thus, it can be stated, either way, the Ishmaelites or the Midianites delivered and sold Joseph to Potiphar in Egypt.

Repetitions (Doublets)

What are doublets? It is the telling of the same story twice, making the same events appear to happen more than once. For example,

(1) there are two stories of the creation account,

(2) two stories of God's covenant with Abraham,

(3) two stories where Abraham names his son Isaac,

(4) two stories where Abraham claims Sarah is his sister, two stories of Jacob's journey to Haran,

(5) two stories where God revealed himself to Jacob at Bethel,

(6) two stories where God changes Jacob's name to Israel,

(7) two stories of when Moses got water from the rock at Meribah, and a detailed description in Exodus 24–29 of how to build the tabernacle, then within five chapters a retelling of how they did it, repeating the details again in chapters 34–40.

The critic goes on to point out that, there is more to this "doublet" story than meets the eye; they argue that one of the doublets will contain the title for the Creator, God (*Elohim*); while the other doublet of the same story will contain the personal name for the Creator, Jehovah. Moreover, they argue that there are other defining features that are only within one side or the other.

> **(Genesis 1:27, ESV)** So God created man in his own image, in the image of God he created him; male and female he created them.

> **(Genesis 2:7, ASV)** And Jehovah God formed man of the dust of the ground, and breathed into his nostrils the breath of life, and man became a living soul.

Within two chapters, we have two verses where the writer, if one person, informs us of the creation of man twice, the second as though the first was never mentioned at all. Again, the source critic will argue that there were two sources of the same information on the creation of man and the compiler allowed both to remain. What the source critic fails to tell his reader is that there are sense breaks within the various accounts in these first three chapters. Genesis 1:1–2:3 is the basic creation account. Genesis 2:4–25 is the restating of day three (verses 5, 6) and the subsequent preparation of the earth for the settling of man and woman in the Garden of Eden. Genesis 3:1–24 is specifically about the temptation, the entry of sin and death into the world, the promise of a seed to save humankind, a description of the conditions of imperfection and of man's loss of the Garden of Eden.

Bible scholar Leon Kass, who supports the Documentary Hypothesis, had this to say about the creation account of Genesis chapters 1 and 2:

> Once we recognize the independence of the two creation stories, we are compelled to adopt a critical principle of reading if we mean to

understand each story on its own terms. We must scrupulously avoid reading into the second story any facts or notions taken from the first, and vice versa. Thus, in reading about the origin of man in the story of the Garden of Eden, we must not say or even think that man is here created in God's image or that man is to be the ruler over the animals. Neither, when we try to understand the relation of man and woman in the Garden, are we to think about or make use of the first story's account of the coequal coeval creation of man and woman. Only after we have read and interpreted each story entirely on its own should we try to integrate the two disparate teachings. By proceeding in this way, we will discover why these two separate and divergent accounts have been juxtaposed and how they function to convey a coherent, noncontradictory teaching about human life.[30]

Let us look at another example in which the critic has argued that one source says forty days while the other speaks of 150 days:

> **(Gen 7:12, NET)** And the rain fell on the earth forty days and forty nights.
>
> **(Gen 7:24, NET)** The waters prevailed over the earth for 150 days.

Genesis 7:24 and 8:3 say the floodwaters lasted for 150 days, yet; Genesis 7:4, 12 and 17 say it was only forty

---

[30] Leon R. Kass, *The Beginning of Wisdom: Reading Genesis* (New York: Free Press, 2003), 56.

days. Once again, the difference is solved with a simple explanation. Each is referring to two different time periods. Let us look at these verses again (italics mine):

> **(Gen 7:12, NET)** And the rain fell on the earth forty days and forty nights. [Notice that the 40-days refer to how long the rain fell—"the rain fell."]
>
> **(Gen 7:24, NET)** The waters prevailed over the earth for 150 days. [Notice that the 150-days refer to how long the flood lasted—"waters prevailed."]
>
> **(Gen 8:3, NET)** The waters kept receding steadily from the earth, so that they had gone down by the end of the 150 days.
>
> **(Gen 8:4, NET)** On the seventeenth day of the seventh month, the ark came to rest on one of the mountains of Ararat.
>
> **(Gen 7:11; 8:13, 14, NET)** In the *six hundredth year of Noah's life,* in *the second month,* on the seventeenth day of the month, on that day all the fountains of the great deep burst open and the floodgates of the heavens were opened. *In Noah's six hundred and first year,* in the first day of the first month, *the waters had dried up* from the earth, and Noah removed the covering from the ark and saw that *the surface of the ground was dry.* And *by the twenty-seventh day of the second month the earth was dry.*

By the end of the 150 days, the water had gone down [Gen 8:3]. Five months from the beginning of the rain, the ark comes to rest on Mount Ararat [8:4]. Eleven months later the waters dried up [7:11; 8:13]. Exactly 370 days from the start (lunar months), Noah and his family left the ark and were on dry ground.

Yet another example is found in 2 Kings 24:10-16. Verses 10-14 say, "At that time the servants of Nebuchadnezzar king of Babylon came up to Jerusalem, and the city was besieged. And Nebuchadnezzar king of Babylon came to the city while his servants were besieging it, and Jehoiachin the king of Judah gave himself up to the king of Babylon, himself and his mother and his servants and his officials and his palace officials. The king of Babylon took him prisoner in the eighth year of his reign and carried off all the treasures of the house of the LORD and the treasures of the king's house, and cut in pieces all the vessels of gold in the temple of the LORD, which Solomon king of Israel had made, as the LORD had foretold. He carried away all Jerusalem and all the officials and all the mighty men of valor, 10,000 captives, and all the craftsmen and the smiths. None remained, except the poorest people of the land."

Verses 15-16 say, "And he carried away Jehoiachin to Babylon. The king's mother, the king's wives, his officials, and the chief men of the land he took into captivity from Jerusalem to Babylon. And the king of Babylon brought captive to Babylon all the men of valor, 7,000, and the craftsmen and the metal workers, 1,000, all of them strong and fit for war."

Here we have a repetition of the same events back-to-back. Why? Is it multiple sources and the redactor simply keeping both? In an attempt to stave off the conservative view of Moses' writership, scholar, and critic Richard Elliot Friedman writes:

> Those who defended the traditional belief in Mosaic authorship argued that the doublets were always complementary, not repetitive and

that they did not contradict each other, but came to teach us a lesson by their 'apparent' contradiction. But another clue was discovered that undermined this traditional response. Investigators found that in most cases one of the two versions of a doublet story would refer to the deity by the divine name, Yahweh . . . , and the other version of the story would refer to the deity simply as 'God.' That is, the doublets lined up into two groups of parallel versions of stories. Each group was almost always consistent with the name it used. Moreover, the investigators found that it was not only the names of the deity that lined up. They found various other terms and characteristics that regularly appeared in one of the other group. This tended to support the hypothesis that someone had taken two different old source documents, cut them up, and woven them together to form the continuous story in the Five Books of Moses.[31]

Ancient Semitic literature has other similar examples of repetition. Moreover, the use of Elohim in one instance and Jehovah in another is due to context and semantic issues. Notice Friedman's use of the phrases "in most cases" and "almost always." Which is it? And as we will see, he is overstating his case to the point of exaggeration. Let us look at the most popular example in the "Matriarch in Danger." It has three occurrences in Genesis: Sarah in Egypt with Pharaoh (Genesis 12:10–20), Sarah in Gerar with Abimelech (Genesis 20:1–18), and Rebekah in Gerar with Abimelech (Genesis 26:7–11). Friedman would argue that we simply have one story with three different sources that had been maintained over time. The personal name of

---

[31] Richard Elliot Friedman, *Who Wrote The Bible* (San Francisco: Harper Collins, 1997), 22.

God, Jehovah, is used in the account of Sarah in Egypt with Pharaoh (vs. 17). The title Elohim is used in the account about Sarah in Gerar with Abimelech (vs. 3), but so is Jehovah (vs. 18). In the account of Rebekah in Gerar with Abimelech, neither Elohim nor Jehovah is used. Therefore, Friedman's case is really no case at all, because both Jehovah and Elohim appear in one account with Sarah in Gerar with Abimelech and neither Jehovah nor Elohim appear in the account with Rebekah in Gerar with Abimelech. It should be noted that all three occurrences are in reference to Abimelech and Pharaoh, but both times that the name Jehovah is used, it is in reference to Jehovah executing a punishment of these rulers. If their best example does not even come close to their claims, then what are we to think of the others? Before moving on to the differences in language and style, we should close with one last point about the literature of the Ancient Near East (ANE). One of the features of ANE literature, which includes Hebrew, is its parallelism, repetition, the telling of stories that are similar to stress patterns that are important. Even in the book of Acts, you have three different accounts of Paul's conversion (Ac 9:3-8; 22:6-11; 26:12-18). It is repetition for emphasis. At the outset of this section, we mentioned that chapters 24-29 of Exodus give a detailed description of how the tabernacle was built, and chapters 34-40 repeat the very same information. Chapters 24-29 contain the directions, and chapters 34-40 show how they did it; thus, the repetition is emphasizing that they did exactly what Jehovah had asked them to do.

Differences in Language and Style

Supporters of the Documentary Hypothesis would argue that within the Pentateuch we see such things as preferences for certain words, differences in vocabulary, reoccurring expressions in Deuteronomy that are not found in Genesis, Exodus, Leviticus, and Numbers, all evidence for the higher critics and their multiple source theory. Also, there are individual characteristics in grammar and syntax. Further, the critic describes "P" as being very boring, completely lacking in interest or excitement, dry; while the writers of "J" and "E" are very vivid and lively, holding the reader's interest in their storytelling. Additionally, "D" uses expressions like 'with all your heart and all your soul,' which the rest of the Pentateuch lacks in those types of expressions. Their conclusion is that there is no alternative but to have multiple writers as the differences in language and style dictate.

If the alleged writers of the Pentateuch were so narrow in their vocabulary and writing abilities that they would use only one given word for a given idea and never use another when dealing with that idea, it would be easy to suggest a division of actual sources. Yet this is not the case at all. The writers of the Hebrew Scriptures throughout ancient Israel actually expressed a great variety of words in their work. Douglas K. Stuart (Ph.D., Harvard University), Professor of Old Testament at Gordon–Conwell Theological Seminary, is of the same opinion:

> In fact, the contrary situation appears to be true. In ancient Israel there were four demonstrable indications of a preference for

variety in written expression rather than for desire for stylistic consistency. (1) If there were two different ways of spelling a word the Israelites chose to preserve both spellings as valid and to include both of them frequently in any document. Thus with regard to spelling (orthography), ancient Israelites had no commitment to consistency to style, but the free use of alternative spellings was regarded as not only proper, but desirable. (2) In the case of common expressions, a similar phenomenon can be observed. Where variation was possible, it apparently was not avoided, but preferred. Alternative ways of forming a given multiword expression were employed commonly so that both alternatives were preserved. Thus, in the case of repeated phraseology in prose contexts, there was no commitment to consistency of style, but rather the alternative formulation was regarded not only proper, but desirable. (3) With regard to variation in grammatical forms, a similar phenomenon is observed. If there existed two different ways of saying something, even in the case of a common verb form, both ways were used so as to preserve both in the common discourse. Again, the preference appears to have been for inclusion of variety rather than for consistency of one form if two existed. (4) The Masoretic system of *Kethib-Qere* represents a fourth indicator of the tendency in past times to preserve variance rather than to select one option and to employ it consistently, a tendency that extended into the medieval period when the Masoretes worked. This system arose from a desire to include, not merely side-by-side, but actually within the same word, two variant readings rather than two select ones. The Masoretes provide the consonants of one text option in the vowels of another. They indicated their preferred reading, but did not omit the reading they regarded as inferior, they simply did not localize it.[32]

Differences in Style and Vocabulary: An investigator would not be honest if he were simply to reject these differences out of hand, as though they did not exist. Therefore, rightly, we need to investigate these differences, giving an answer that has substance. I will cite one of their pillar examples, to demonstrate the principle that if they are so far off base here, then we can conclude their foundation in this area is really no foundation at all. Before we get started, let us do a little review of Biblical Hebrew, to be better able to address our example.

> **(Qal):** Qal is the simple form of the verb, meaning "light" or "easy." This is the simple active stem of the verb.
>
> **(Hiphil):** This is generally called the "*causative*" form because it reveals the *causative* action of the qal verb. The "*h*" is prefixed to the stem, which modifies the root.

QAL	yalad (to give birth)
HIPHIL	holid (he caused to give birth)

---

[32] Douglas K. Stuart, *The New American Commentary: An Exegetical Theological Exposition of Holy Scripture: EXODUS* (Nashville: Broadman & Holman, 2006). See pp. 30–31 for examples of the above four points.

Examples:

> **Gen. 14:18**: Irad begat (*yalad*) Mehujael
>
> **Gen. 5:4**: Adam after he begat (*holid*) Seth

The advocates of the Documentary Hypothesis argue that to find *yalad* in the genealogy of Cain in Genesis chapter 4, the Table of Nations in Genesis chapter 10, and Nahor's family line in Genesis chapter 22 (all being of the "J" author), while finding *holid* in Adam's history down to Noah in Genesis chapter 5 as well as the genealogy of Shem found in Genesis chapter 11 (being of the "P" author) is nothing more than proof positive that there are two authors: "J" and "P."

In short, we are not dealing with a word or phrase that is peculiar to an individual writer like "J" or "P." No, this is nothing more than an example of following the basic rules of Hebrew grammar and syntax. In many cases, it could not have been written in any other way, because it is the socially accepted usage of the Hebrew language. When those who support the Documentary Hypothesis pull Hebrew words or even phrases out of their setting (as I have done above), looking at them in isolation, their reasoning becomes based solely on personal wishes, feelings, or perceptions, rather than on linguistic rules, reasons, or principles of the language itself. Hebrew, like any other language, conforms to the socially accepted style, with the regular and specific order, or arrangement. The Hebrew language has its own rules and allowable combinations of how words are joined together to make sense to the Hebrew mind. Umberto Cassuto, also known as Moshe David Cassuto, (1883–1951), who held the chair of Biblical studies at the Hebrew University of Jerusalem had this to say concerning the usage of *yalad* and *holid:*

It will suffice to note the fact that the verb *yaladh* occurs in the signification of *holidh* only in the *past tense* [perfect] and the *present* [participle]. We say, "so-and-so *yaladh* [mas. sing. perfect] so-and-so," and we say *yoledh* [participle mas. Sing.: "is begetting"]; but we do not say in the *future tense* [imperfect] so-and-so *yeledh* [to signify: "he will beget"] (or *wayyeledh* [imperfect with *waw* conversive, to connote: "and he begot"]) so-and-so." In the imperfect, the *Qal* is employed only with reference to the mother, for example, so-and-so *teledh* ["will give birth to"] (*watteledh* ["and gave birth to"]) so and so." In connection with the father one can only say, *yolidh* [hiphil imperfect; "he will beget"] or *wayyoledh* [hiphil imperfect with *waw* conversive; "and he begot"] (although we find in Prov. xxvii 1: what a day may bring forth ["*yeledh*"; *Qal* imperfect] the verb is used there not in connotation of "begetting" but actually in the sense of "giving birth"). Similarly, we do not say, using the infinitive, Aajare *lidhto* [to signify: "after his begetting"] but only Aajare *lidhtah* ["after her giving birth"]; with regard to the father we can only say Aajare *holidho* ["after his begetting"]. This is clear to anyone who is sensitive to the Hebrew idiom. In the genealogies from Adam to Noah and from Noah to Abraham, it would have been impossible to write anything else but *wayyoledh* and Aajare *hoilidho;* every Hebrew author would have had no option but to write thus and not otherwise. It is not a question of sources but of the general usage of the Hebrew tongue.[33]

Professor K. A. Kitchen, one of the leading experts on Biblical history, notes in his book *Ancient Orient and Old Testament:* "Stylistic differences are meaningless, and reflect the differences in detailed subject-matter." He says that similar style variations can also be found "in ancient texts whose literary unity is beyond all doubt."[34]

A 1981 news report relates to this debate and provides some interesting facts.[35]

> TEL AVIV, Israel (UPI)—A five-year-long computer study of the Bible strongly indicates that one author—and not three as widely held in modern criticism—wrote the book of Genesis.
>
> "The probability of Genesis' having been written by one author is enormously high—82 percent statistically," a member of the research team said in an article published in Wednesday's *Jerusalem Post.*
>
> Professor Yehuda Radday, a Bible scholar from the Technion, a Haifa University, said more than 20,000 words of Genesis were fed into a computer which conducted a painstaking analysis of its linguistic makeup.
>
> Bible critics widely hold that Genesis had three authors—the Jawhist or "J" author, the

---

[33] Umberto Cassuto, *The Documentary Hypothesis* (New York, NY: Shalem Press, 2006), 55-56.

[34] K. A Kitchen, *Ancient Orient and Old Testament* (Downers Grove, IL: InterVarsity Press, 1975), 125.

[35] As published in the *St. Petersburg Times:* http://tinyurl.com/noke4m

Elohist or "E" author and a priestly writer, dubbed "P."

"We found the J and E narratives to be linguistically indistinguishable," Radday told a news conference today. But the P sections differ widely from them.

"This is only to be expected, since dramatic tales and legal documents must necessarily display different 'behavior,'" he said. "If you compared love letters and a telephone directory written by the same person, linguistic analysis would point to different authors."

The team combined statistical and linguistic methods with computer science and Bible scholarship to reach their conclusions. They used 54 analysis criteria, including word length, the use of the definite article and the conjunction "and," richness of vocabulary and transition frequencies between word categories.

"These criteria are a reliable gauge of authorship because these traits are beyond an author's conscious control and furthermore are countable," Radday said.

A mathematics expert on the team ran a computer check against classical German works by Goethe, Herder and Kant and found that the statistical probability of their being the sole authors of their own work were only 22 percent, 7 percent and 9 percent respectively.

As mentioned above, Jewish and Christian conservatives accept one writer for the first five books of the Bible, namely, Moses. The critics, however, argue that although Moses is definitely the main character of the Pentateuch because they are unable to find any *direct mention* within it of Moses having written these five books, it is for them simply a tradition that Moses is the writer. This author is certain that is not the impression you will have after reading the next chapter.

Internal and External Evidence for Moses Authorship

First, it is obvious that Moses did *not* write *every word* of the Pentateuch. Why? The section that relates his death would be something that Joshua could have added after Moses' death. (Deuteronomy 34:1–8) In addition, the critic would argue, it would hardly seem very meek to pen these words about oneself: "Now the man Moses was very meek, more than all people who were on the face of the earth." (Numbers 12:3, ESV) Nevertheless, consider that Jesus said of himself: "I am gentle and lowly in heart" (Matthew 11:29, *ESV*), which no one would fault Jesus with as though he were boasting. Both Moses and Jesus were simply stating a fact. The amount of possible material that may have been added by Joshua, another inspired writer is next to nothing and does not negate Moses' authorship.

What Does the Biblical Evidence from the Old Testament Report?

Exodus 17:14 (ASV)	Exodus 24:4 (ASV)	Exodus 34:27 (ASV)
14 And Jehovah said unto Moses, Write this for a memorial in a book, and rehearse it in the ears of Joshua: that I will utterly blot out the	4 And Moses wrote all the words of Jehovah, and rose up early in the morning, and builded an altar under the mount, and twelve	27 And Jehovah said unto Moses, Write thou these words: for after the tenor of these words I have made a covenant with

remembrance of Amalek from under heaven.	pillars, according to the twelve tribes of Israel.	thee and with Israel.
Leviticus 26:46 (ASV) ⁴⁶ These are the statutes and ordinances and laws, which Jehovah made between him and the children of Israel in mount Sinai by Moses.	**Leviticus 27:34 (ASV)** ³⁴ These are the commandments, which Jehovah commanded Moses for the children of Israel in mount Sinai.	**Numbers 33:2 (ASV)** ² And Moses wrote their goings out according to their journeys by the commandment of Jehovah: and these are their journeys according to their goings out.
Numbers 36:13 (ASV) ¹³ These are the commandments and the ordinances which Jehovah commanded by Moses unto the children of Israel in the plains of Moab by the Jordan at Jericho.	**Deuteronomy 1:1 (ASV)** ¹ These are the words which Moses spake unto all Israel beyond the Jordan in the wilderness, in the Arabah over against Suph, between Paran, and Tophel, and Laban, and	**Deuteronomy 31:9 (ASV)** ⁹ And Moses wrote this law, and delivered it unto the priests the sons of Levi, that bare the ark of the covenant of Jehovah, and unto all the elders of Israel.

	Hazeroth, and Di-zahab.	
Deuteronomy 31:22 (ASV) ²² So Moses wrote this song the same day, and taught it the children of Israel.	**Deuteronomy 31:24 (ASV)** ²⁴ And it came to pass, when Moses had made an end of writing the words of this law in a book, until they were finished,	**Joshua 1:7 (ASV)** ⁷ Only be strong and very courageous, to observe to do according to all the law, which Moses my servant commanded thee:
Joshua 8:31 (ASV) ³¹ as Moses the servant of Jehovah commanded the children of Israel, as it is written in the book of the law of Moses, an altar of unhewn stones, upon which no man had lifted up any iron: and they offered thereon burnt-offerings unto	**1 Kings 2:3 (ASV)** ³ and keep the charge of Jehovah thy God, to walk in his ways, to keep his statutes, and his commandments, and his ordinances, and his testimonies, according to that which is written in the law of Moses, that thou may prosper in all that thou does, and	**2 Kings 14:6 (ASV)** ⁶ but the children of the murderers he put not to death; according to that which is written in the book of the law of Moses, as Jehovah commanded, saying, The fathers shall not be put to death for the children, nor the children

Jehovah, and sacrificed peace-offerings.	whithersoever thou turn thyself.	be put to death for the fathers; but every man shall die for his own sin.
2 Kings 21:8 (ASV) ⁸ neither will I cause the feet of Israel to wander any more out of the land which I gave their fathers, if only they will observe to do according to all that I have commanded them, and according to all the law that my servant Moses commanded them.	**Ezra 6:18 (ASV)** ¹⁸ And they set the priests in their divisions, and the Levites in their courses, for the service of God, which is at Jerusalem; as it is written in the book of Moses.	**Nehemiah 13:1 (ASV)** ¹ On that day they read in the book of Moses in the audience of the people; and therein was found written, that an Ammonite and a Moabite should not enter into the assembly of God for ever,
Daniel 9:13 (ASV) ¹³ As it is written in the law of Moses, all this evil is come upon us: yet have we not	**Malachi 4:4 (ASV)** ⁴ Remember ye the law of Moses my servant, which I commanded unto him in	

entreated the favor of Jehovah our God, that ...	Horeb for all Israel, even statutes and ordinances.	

To reject Moses as the writer of the Pentateuch is to reject these inspired writers and suggest they are not reliable; moreover, this would mean they were not inspired, because those under inspiration would not make such errors. If these critics are correct, then all the above is merely a great conspiracy. This author hardly thinks so!

What Does the Biblical Evidence from Jesus Christ Report?

Matthew 8:4 (ESV)	Matthew 11:23-24 (ESV)
[4] And Jesus said to him, "See that you say nothing to anyone, but go, show yourself to the priest and offer the gift that Moses commanded, for a proof to them."	[23] And you, Capernaum, will you be exalted to heaven? You will be brought down to Hades. For if the mighty works done in you had been done in Sodom, it would have remained until this day. [24] But I tell you that it will be more tolerable on the day of judgment for the land of Sodom than for you."
Matthew 19:4-5 (ESV)	Matthew 19:8 (ESV)
[4] He answered, "Have you not read that he who created them from the	[8] He said to them, "Because of your hardness of heart Moses allowed you to

beginning made them male and female, ⁵and said, 'Therefore a man shall leave his father and his mother and hold fast to his wife, and the two shall become one flesh'?

divorce your wives, but from the beginning it was not so.

Matthew 24:37 (ESV)

³⁷ For as were the days of Noah, so will be the coming of the Son of Man.

Mark 10:5 (ESV)

⁵And Jesus said to them, "Because of your hardness of heart he wrote you this commandment.

Mark 12:26 (ESV)

²⁶And as for the dead being raised, have you not read in the book of Moses, in the passage about the bush, how God spoke to him, saying, 'I am the God of Abraham, and the God of Isaac, and the God of Jacob'?

Mark 1:44 (ESV)

⁴⁴and said to him, "See that you say nothing to anyone, but go, show yourself to the priest and offer for your cleansing what Moses commanded, for a proof to them."

Mark 7:10 (ESV)

¹⁰For Moses said, 'Honor your father and your mother'; and, 'Whoever reviles father or mother must surely die.'

Luke 5:14 (ESV)

¹⁴And he charged him to tell no one, but "go and show yourself to the priest, and make an offering for your cleansing, as Moses commanded, for a proof to them."

Luke 11:51 (ESV)	Luke 17:32 (ESV)
⁵¹from the blood of Abel to the blood of Zechariah, who perished between the altar and the sanctuary. Yes, I tell you, it will be required of this generation.	³² Remember Lot's wife.
Luke 24:27, 44 English Standard Version (ESV) ²⁷And beginning with Moses and all the Prophets, he interpreted to them in all the Scriptures the things concerning himself. ⁴⁴Then he said to them, "These are my words that I spoke to you while I was still with you, that everything written about me in the Law of Moses and the Prophets and the Psalms must be fulfilled."	**John 5:46 English Standard Version (ESV)** ⁴⁶For if you believed Moses, you would believe me; for he wrote of me.
John 7:19 English Standard Version (ESV) ¹⁹ Has not Moses given you the law? Yet none of	**John 8:58 (UASV)** Jesus said to them, "Truly, truly, I say to you, before Abraham came to be I have been in existence."[36]

---

[36] K. L. McKay, A New Syntax of the Verb in New Testament Greek (New York: Peter Lang, 1994), p. 42.

you keeps the law. Why do you seek to kill me?"	

How does one ignore the strongest evidence of Moses' writership of these five books, which is specifically referred to by Jesus Christ and numerous other inspired writers? Being on trial by the modern day critic, I am certain Moses would appreciate the numerous witnesses that can be called to the stand on his behalf.[37]

What Does the Biblical Evidence from the Apostles Report?

Acts 2:32 (ESV)	Acts 6:14 (ESV)	Acts 15:5 (ESV)
[32]This Jesus God raised up, and of that we all are witnesses.	[14]for we have heard him say that this Jesus of Nazareth will destroy this place and will change the customs that Moses delivered to us."	[5]But some believers who belonged to the party of the Pharisees rose up and said, "It is necessary to circumcise them and to order them to keep the law of Moses."

---

[37] Old Testament witnesses to Moses' writership of the Pentateuch: Joshua 1:7; 8:32–35; 14:10; 1 Kings 2:3; 1 Chronicles 6:49; 2 Chronicles 33:8; 34:14; 35:12; Ezra 3:2; 6:18; 7:6; Nehemiah 1:7, 8; 8:1, 14, 15; Daniel 9:11, 13; Malachi 4:4. New Testament witnesses to Moses' writership of the Pentateuch: Matthew 8:2–4; 19:7; Mark 1:44; 12:26; Luke 2:22; 16:29, 31; 24:27, 44; John 1:45; 7:22; 8:5; 9:29; 19:7 [Leviticus 24:16]; Acts 3:22; 6:14; 15:5; 26:22; 28:23; Romans 10:5; 1 Corinthians 9:9; Hebrews 9:19; 10:28.

Acts 26:22 (ESV)	Acts 28:23 (ESV)	Romans 10:5 (ESV)
²² To this day I have had the help that comes from God, and so I stand here testifying both to small and great, saying nothing but what the prophets and Moses said would come to pass:	²³When they had appointed a day for him, they came to him at his lodging in greater numbers. From morning till evening he expounded to them, testifying to the kingdom of God and trying to convince them about Jesus both from the Law of Moses and from the Prophets.	⁵For Moses writes about the righteousness that is based on the law, that the person who does the commandments shall live by them.
1 Corinthians 9:9 (ESV)	Hebrews 9:19 (ESV)	Hebrews 10:28 (ESV)
⁹For it is written in the Law of Moses, "You shall not muzzle an ox when it treads out the grain." Is it for oxen that God is concerned?	¹⁹For when every commandment of the law had been declared by Moses to all the people, he took the blood of calves and ...	²⁸ Anyone who has set aside the law of Moses dies without mercy on the evidence of two or three witnesses.

What Does the Internal Evidence Report?

If the writer(s) of the Pentateuch were, in fact, living from the ninth century into the fifth century B.C.E., more than a millennium [1,000 years] after the events described, they would have had to be thoroughly familiar with, even an expert in geology, geography,[38] horticulture, archaeology, toponymy, onomatology (Archer, 1974), botany, zoology,[39] climatology,[40] and history. **Alternatively**, he would have to have been an eyewitness who walked through the events and situations detailed in the Pentateuch; thus, the writer. Here is how I defend these affirmations:

- He would need to have a thorough knowledge of Egyptian names and titles that match inscriptions.

- He would need to have been an expert in toponymy, the study of place-names.

- He would need to have been an expert in onomatology, the study of proper names of all kinds and the origin of names.

- He would need to be aware of the customs and cultures and religious practices of Egypt, desert dwellers, and life in Canaan 1,000 years into the past.

- He would need to have a thorough knowledge of the environment, climate, and the physical features of three regions.

---

[38] Genesis 13:10; 33:18; Numbers 13:22.

[39] Leviticus 11 and Deuteronomy 14.

[40] Exodus 9:31, 32; Exodus 16–Deuteronomy.

- He would need to have a thorough knowledge of botany, being aware of naturally occurring plant life in three regions 1,000-years before his time.
- He would need to have a thorough knowledge of the environment, climate, and the physical features of three regions.

This internal evidence deals with the proof within the Pentateuch about Moses: the customs and culture of some 3,500 years ago, literary forms used as well as the language itself, and the unity of these five books. As to dating the Pentateuch based on literary forms, one needs to look no further than the titles of which God is referred to within the Hebrew Scriptures. From the years of 850–450 B.C.E., we find the Hebrew expression *Yehowah´ tseva'ohth´,* "Jehovah of armies," being used in a significant way. It is found 243 times, with variations, in the Scriptures: 62 times in Isaiah, 77 in Jeremiah, 2 in Micah, 4 in Nahum, 2 in Habakkuk, 2 in Zephaniah, 15 in Haggai, 54 in Zechariah, and 25 in Malachi. This is the same time period, in which higher criticism places the writing of the books of the Pentateuch. If they were penned or constructed during this time period, one would expect to find a high number of occurrences of the expression "Jehovah of armies." Yet, we find just the opposite: there is not one occurrence of this expression to be found in the five books of the Pentateuch. This evidence demonstrates that these books were written prior to the book of Isaiah, before 800 B.C.E., which invalidates the Documentary Hypothesis. Moreover, many aspects of the priesthood that had been adjusted over the centuries, under inspiration, would have been evident if the Pentateuch were written after David[41] and others had made such adjustments.

The building of the tabernacle at the foot of Mount Sinai fits in with the environment of that area. F. C. Cook stated, "In form, structure, and materials, the tabernacle belongs altogether to the wilderness. The wood used in the structure is found there in abundance."[42] The external evidence validates names, customs, and culture, religious practices, geography, places and materials of the book of Exodus, which would have been privy only to an eyewitness. The geographical references by this writer are so vast, detailed, and tremendously precise that it is almost impossible to have him be anyone other than an eyewitness.

Deuteronomy reads, "Then we . . . went through all that great and terrifying wilderness." This region in which the annual rainfall is less than 25 cm./10 in. is not different even today, which puts the nomadic traveler on a constant search for water and pasture. In addition, we have meticulous directions as to the encampment of the Israelites (Numbers 1:52, 53), the marching orders (Numbers 2:9, 16, 17, 24, 31), and the signals of the trumpet (Numbers 10:2–6) that directed their every move as evidence that these accounts were written in the "great and terrifying wilderness." Numbers 13:22 makes reference to the time Hebron was built, using the city of Zoan as a reference point: "They went up into the Negeb and came to Hebron. Ahiman, Sheshai, and Talmai, the descendants of Anak, were there. (Hebron was built seven years before Zoan in Egypt.)" Moses "was instructed in all

---

[41] David organized the tens of thousands of Levites into their many divisions of service, including a great chorus of singers and musicians.—1 Chronicles 23:1–29:19; 2 Chronicles 8:14; 23:18; 29:25; Ezra 3:10.

[42] F. C. Cook, *Exodus* (1874), 247.

the wisdom of the Egyptians" (Acts 7:22); thus, he would have knowledge of the building of Zoan, an Egyptian city, and of Hebron, a city on one of the trade routes between Memphis in Egypt and Damascus in Syria.

From the internal evidence, it is clearly obvious that the writer must have had an intimate knowledge of the desert, being an eyewitness to that environment. (See Leviticus 18:3; Deuteronomy 12:9; 15:4, 7; Numbers 2:1; Leviticus 14:8; 16:21; 17:3, 9.) The evidence is such because it is something that cannot be retained for a thousand years, but must come from an eyewitness. The details are extremely exact, and some would not have existed hundreds of years later: "Then they came to Elim, where there were twelve wells of water and seventy palm trees, and they camped there by the water," and "ram skins dyed red, fine leather, acacia wood." – Exodus 15:27; 25:5

Again, it should be noted that Moses "was instructed in all the wisdom of the Egyptians." (Acts 7:22) It is also obvious that the writer was quite familiar with Egyptian names: Pithom, meaning "House of Atum;" On, meaning "City of the Pillar" (the Greeks called the city Heliopolis); Potiphera,[43] meaning "He Whom Ra Has Given;" and Asenath, her name deriving from Egyptian, meaning: "Holy to Anath."

In addition, the writer used Egyptian words generously. "He had Joseph ride in his second chariot, and [servants] called out before him, '*Abrek!*' So he placed him over all the land of Egypt." (Genesis 41:43) The exact meaning of this expression transliterated from Egyptian into Hebrew has not yet been determined. Some feel that it is an Egyptian word meaning (*Attention!*) while others see it as a Hebrew word meaning *Kneel* or *Bow down!*

---

[43] A funeral pillar (stele) discovered in 1935 and now in the Cairo Museum refers to a personage named Potiphare.

One misstep and the writer will lose credibility. However, this is never the case with the writer of the Pentateuch. He mentions the acacia tree, which is found in Egypt and Sinai but not in the land of Canaan. Moreover, this writer refers to numerous animals that are to be found primarily in Egypt or Sinai. – See Deuteronomy. 14:5; Leviticus 16:11.

The old form of words in the Pentateuch are of the time frame of the fifteenth century B.C.E. as well and had no longer been in use for centuries by the time of the supposed writer(s) and redactor(s) of the ninth to the sixth centuries B.C.E. Dr. John J. Davis gives us the most widely recognized example, "The pronoun *she*, which appears as *hiw'* instead of *hî'*. Another example is the word *young girl*, spelled *na'ar* instead of *na'ărâ*, the feminine form."[44]

All who engaged in idolatry or prophesying falsely were to be stoned to death, no exceptions. (Deuteronomy 13:2–11) This included not only individuals but also entire communities, every person within a city (verses 12–17). One has to ask, why would a writer include this if it were penned during the time period of 850–450 B.C.E. when most of the time Israel was shoulder deep in idolatry and false prophets abounded? This would mean certain destruction for every city in the kingdom. It would have been mere foolishness to incorporate these laws, which could never be enforced and would cause nothing but resistance to the law. However, it makes perfectly good sense for laws such as these to be given to people living in the time of Moses who had just exited an idolatrous nation and who was preparing to go in and conquer a number of other nations who lived and breathed idolatry.

---

[44] John J. Davis, *Paradise to Prison: Studies in Genesis* (Salem: Sheffield, 1975), 26.

What Does the External Evidence Report?

"The book of the law of Moses," as Joshua called the Pentateuch, was accepted by Jews, Christians, and Muslims as containing evidence of inspiration. The fact that Moses is the writer of these five books is **not** something that grew up out of tradition; it is something Moses himself claims, saying he wrote under the divine command of Jehovah God. Moreover, the Jewish communities throughout the Roman empire were in total harmony with the fact that Moses was the writer of the Pentateuch, this being supported by the Samaritan Pentateuch, the Palestinian Talmud, the Babylonian Talmud, the Apocrypha, Philo Judaeus (a contemporary of Jesus and Paul and the first century), and by Jewish historian Flavius Josephus (37–100 C.E.).[45] What about the early Christian writers, who wrote about Christianity between 150 C.E. and 400 C.E.?

> Moses, the servant of God, recorded, through the Holy Spirit, the very beginning of the creation of the world. First he spoke of the things concerning the creation and genesis of the world, including the first man and everything that happened afterwards in the order of events. He also indicated the number of years that elapsed before the Deluge. – *Theophilus* (c. 180, E), 2.118.[46]

> The origin of that knowledge should not, on that account, be considered as originating with the Pentateuch. For knowledge of the Creator did not begin with the volume of Moses.

---

[45] See Ecclesiasticus 45:5; 2 Maccabees 7:30; Philo (*On the Life of Moses* II; III, 12–14; IV, 20; VIII, 45–48, pp. 93–95); Josephus (*The Antiquities of the Jews*, 3.8.10); Exodus 17:14; 24:4.

[46] David W. Bercot, A *Dictionary of Early Christian Beliefs* (Peabody: Hendrickson, 1998), 599.

Rather from the very first it is traced from Adam and paradise.—*Tertullian* (c. 207, W), 3.278.[47]

What portion of scripture can give us more information concerning the creation of the world than the account that Moses has transmitted? – *Origen* (c. 225, E), 4.341.[48]

The destruction of Sodom and Gomorrah by fire on account of their sins is related by Moses in Genesis. – *Origen* (c. 248, E), 4.505.[49]

Moses said, "And the Lord God saw that the wickedness of men was overflowing upon the Earth" [Gen. 6:5–7]. – *Novatian* (c. 235, W), 5.658.[50]

It is contained in the book of Moses, which he wrote about creation, in which is called Genesis. – *Victorinus* (c. 280, W), 7.341.[51]

If you will look at the books of Moses, David, Solomon, Isaiah, or the Prophets who follow . . . . You will see what offspring they have left. – *Methodious* (c. 290, E), 6.333.[52]

Let the following books be considered venerable and holy by you, both of the clergy and the laity. Of the Old Testament: The five books of Moses—Genesis, Exodus, Leviticus, Numbers, and Deuteronomy. . . .--*Apostolic Constitutions* (compiled c. 390, E), 7.505.[53]

---

47. Ibid., 600.
48. Ibid., 600.
49. Ibid., 600.
50. Ibid., 601.
51. Ibid., 601.
52. Ibid., 601.
53. Ibid., 602.

Archaeology and the Bible

Unlike higher criticism, archaeology is a field of study that has a solid foundation in physical evidence, instead of presenting only hypotheses, inferences, and implications. Within archaeology, one has both explicit and direct evidence as well as implicit evidence. There are many great publications that will undoubtedly go into this area in much greater detail, but suffice it to say that the Biblical events, the characters, geography, agriculture, plants and trees, and settings are all in harmony with and accessible through archaeology.

While archaeology is not a total vindicator, it has defended God's Word. No one can argue against the fact that our understanding of ancient times has increased tremendously over the past 150 years and is being continuously refined. At present, one could list thousands of events within the Scriptures that are in complete harmony with the archaeological record. In fact, Wellhausen had nothing like what is available to the modern scholar. If he had, one would have to wonder if he would have come to the same conclusions. Conveying this exact point, Dr. Mark F. Rooker, Professor of Old Testament and Hebrew, stated:

> Regarding the issue of differing divine names, it is now clear from archaeological data not available to Wellhausen and early critical scholars that deities in the ancient Near East often had multiple names. This fact is especially clear in the conclusion to the Babylonian Creation account, the *Enuma Elish,* where the god Marduk is declared to be preeminent and his fifty different names are mentioned in celebration of his conquest.[22] No one has

suggested that each name represents a different source, as was done in biblical studies. On the contrary, it would have been impossible to attribute these different names to different sources that have been pasted or joined together in the literary account because the Mesopotamian writing system involved inscription in stone! Moreover, it is clear that throughout the Old Testament the occurrence of the names of God as Elohim or Yahweh are to be attributed to contextual and semantic issues, not the existence of sources. This conclusion is borne out by the fact that the names consistently occur in predictable genre.... Thus through scientific discovery and analysis the criterion of the differing divine names, which gave rise to the Documentary Hypothesis, has been found wanting. If this information would have been known in the last years of the nineteenth century, it is safe to assume that the critical approach to the Pentateuch would never have seen the light of day.[54]

Much archaeological evidence, as well as other forms of evidence, has been uncovered to reveal the accuracy of the record. The ziggurat located at Uruk (Erech) was found to be built with clay, baked bricks for stone, and asphalt (bitumen) for mortar.[55] The Egyptian names and titles that Moses penned in the book of Exodus match Egyptian inscriptions. The book of Exodus shows that the Hebrew people were allowed to live in the land of Egypt as

---

54. Mark F. Rooker, *Leviticus: The New American Commentary* (Nashville: Broadman & Holman, 2001), 26–27.

[55] (Genesis 11:3, *ESV*) "And they said to one another, 'Come, let us make bricks, and burn them thoroughly.' And they had brick for stone, and bitumen for mortar."

foreigners, as long as they kept separate from the Egyptians. Archaeology supports this custom. Likely, you will recall that Pharaoh's daughter bathed in the Nile (Exodus 2:5), which "was a common practice in ancient Egypt," according to Cook's *Commentary.* "The Nile was worshipped as an emanation . . . of Osiris, and a peculiar power of imparting life and fertility was attributed to its waters."

> The fact that a king's daughter should bathe in the open river is certainly opposed to the customs of the modern, Mohammedan East, where this is only done by women of the lower orders, and that in remote places (Lane, *Manners and Customs*); but it is in harmony with the customs of ancient Egypt,[56]* and in perfect agreement with the notions of the early Egyptians respecting the sanctity of the Nile, to which divine honours even were paid (vid., Hengstenberg's *Egypt,* etc. pp. 109, 110), and with the belief, which was common to both ancient and modern Egyptians, in the power of its waters to impart fruitfulness and prolong life (vid., *Strabo,* xv. p. 695, etc., and Seetzen, *Travels* iii. p. 204).[57]

In addition, history also testifies to the fact that magicians were a well-known feature of Egyptian life during the period of Moses. – Genesis 11:1-9; Exodus 8:22; 2:5; 5:6, 7, 18; 7:11.

Bricks have been found made with and without straw. The painting below was found in the private tomb

---

[56] Wilkinson gave a picture of a bathing scene in which an Egyptian woman of rank is introduced, attended by four female servants.

57. Carl Friedric Keil and Franz Delitzsch, *Commentary on the Old Testament* (Peabody, MA: Hendrickson, 2002), S. 1:278.

of Vizier Rekhmire (the highest official under Pharaoh) on the west bank of ancient Thebes. Archaeology also supports "taskmasters--Egyptian overseers, appointed to exact labor of the Israelites,"[58] as well as strictly controlled or enforced quotas that had to be met. (Exodus 5:6) Moreover, Egyptian papyri express serious concern for the needed straw (which was lacking at times) to be mixed with the mud to make these bricks. (Exodus 1:13, 14) The Papyri Anastasi, from ancient Egypt, reads, "There was no one to mould bricks, and there was no straw in the neighbourhood."[59]

Furthermore, the historical conditions and surroundings are in accord precisely with the occasions and assertions in the book of Numbers. We have references to Edom, Egypt, Moab, Canaan, Ammon, and Amalek, which are true to the times, and the names of places are free from error.[60] Archaeology is never absolute proof of anything, but it continues to add evidence, weighty at times to the fact that Moses had to be the writer of the Pentateuch. *Halley's Bible Handbook* writes, "Archaeology has been speaking so loudly of late that it is causing a decided reaction toward the conservative view. The theory that writing was unknown in Moses' day is absolutely exploded. And every year there are being dug up in Egypt, Palestine and Mesopotamia, pieces of evidence, both in inscriptions and earth layers, that the narratives of the Old Testament are true historical records. And 'scholarship' is

---

58. Robert Jamieson, A. R. Fausset, and David Brown. *A Commentary, Critical and Explanatory, On the Old and New Testaments* (Oak Harbor: Scranton & Company, 1997), 51.

59. Adolf Erman and H. M. Tirard. *Life in Ancient Egypt* (Whitefish: Kessinger, 2003), 117.

60. "Sirion . . . Senir." These names appear in the Ugaritic texts found at Ras Shamra, Syria, and in the documents from Bogazköy, Turkey.

coming to have decidedly more respect for the tradition of Mosaic authorship."[61]

The Silver Amulet is one of many archaeological nails in the coffin of the Documentary Hypothesis. Why? This portion of Numbers is argued by the critics to be part of the "P" document that was supposedly penned between 550 and 400 B.C.E. However, initially, it was dated to the late seventh / early sixth centuries B.C.E.

Of course, this dating was subsequently challenged by Johannes Renz and Wolfgang Rollig (*Handbuch der Althebraischen Epigraphik*, 1995) because the silver was cracked and blemished to the point of making many words and a few lines unreadable. This allowed these critics to argue for a date in the third to second centuries B.C.E. period, which would remove this stain on the lifeless body of their Documentary Hypothesis.

Then it was shipped to the University of Southern California to be examined under photographic and computer imaging. The results? The researchers stated that they could "read fully and [had] analyzed with far greater precision," which resulted in the final analysis of being yet another vindication for Moses—the original dating stands late seventh-century B.C.E.

Exodus 14:6, 7 (*ESV*) reads, "So he [the Pharaoh] made ready his chariot and took his army with him and took six hundred chosen chariots and all the other chariots of Egypt with officers over all of them." Pharaoh, being the god of the world and the supreme chief of his army, personally led the army into battle. Archaeology supports this custom.

---

61. Henry Halley, *Halley's Bible Handbook* (Grand Rapids: Zondervan, 1988), 56.

Why are there no Egyptian records of the Exodus of the Israelites from Egypt? The critics may also ask why there is no archaeological evidence to support the Israelite's 215-year stay in Egypt (some of which was in slavery) and the devastation that was executed on the gods of Egypt. There is, in fact, one simple answer that archaeology has provided us: Any new Egyptian dynasty would erase any unflattering history prior to their dynasty, if such even existed, as it was their custom never to record any defeats that might be viewed as embarrassing or critical, which could damage the dignity of their people, for they were an extremely prideful empire.[62]

For example, Thutmose III ordered others to chisel Queen Hatshepsut out of the history books when he removed the name and representation of Queen Hatshepsut on a monumental stone record later uncovered at Deir al-Bahri in Egypt as well as from any other monuments she had built. Hatshepsut, daughter of Thutmose I, would eventually gain the throne upon her father's death even though Thutmose II (husband and half-brother to Hatshepsut) technically ascended the throne in name only. At best, Thutmose II lasted only three or four years before dying of skin disease. Thutmose III was too young to rule. Thus, Queen Hatshepsut simply held her own as the first female Pharaoh. Embarrassing for Thutmose III, indeed! Thus, as he grew, his hatred mounted for Hatshepsut and Senmut (her lover). After her death, Thutmose III worked vigorously to remove her name and the name of her lover from Egyptian history. If this was embarrassing, how much more so would be the ten plagues that had humiliated numerous gods of Egypt, including the Pharaoh himself? The exodus of 600,000 male slaves and their families, plus Egyptians who had

---

62. Joseph P. Free, *Archaeology and Bible History* (Grand Rapids, MI: Zondervan Publishing, 1964).

chosen Jehovah as God instead of the Pharaoh of Egypt would have been quite embarrassing, indeed!

In 1925, discoveries of clay tablets were made at the ancient town of Nuzi in northeastern Mesopotamia; it was here that archaeologists found a tremendous number of legal contracts dating to the fifteenth-century B.C.E. These actually shed much light on the life of people of that time. Due to the slow-moving life condition of the ancient Near East, they reflect life conditions for many years on both sides of the fifteenth century. Thus, what we now possess and know from studies of these Nuzi Tablets is that there are numerous customs in the Patriarchal period that were very much in common practice among the ancient Hurrians who lived in northern Mesopotamia, encompassing Haran, which was the home of Abraham after he left Ur and where Isaac later found his wife, Rebekah.

Abraham's Contract. Eliezer was to be the legal inheritor of childless Abraham's property and position after Abraham's death. In fact, Abraham referred to Eliezer when he said, "a slave born in my house will be my heir." (Genesis 15:2, 3) Tablets from Nuzi discovered by archaeologists help the modern-day reader understand how a servant could become heir to his master's household. Mesopotamian records from the time of Abraham (2018–1843 B.C.E.); makes mention of the tradition of a childless couple adopting a son in their old age to have him take care of them up unto their death, and thereafter inheriting the household property. But if for some reason the couple would end up having a child, the child would become the primary heir instead, with the adopted servant or son getting a minor portion of the property as well. (Wood, 1996) In a culture that passed history down orally through its generations, we find Moses being only three generations removed from Abraham's great-grandson Levi (Levi, Kohath, Amram, and Moses) while our alleged "J" was a thousand years removed from Abraham, and the redactor even further. It is only by means of modern-day archaeology that we are aware of just how accurate the Genesis account is with minor details such as the legal system of adoption rights in Mesopotamia from 2000 B.C.E. (time of Abraham) to 1500 B.C.E. (time of Moses), knowledge that would not be available to our alleged composers. Thus, archaeology puts the Genesis account right back into the hands of its true writer, Moses.

The Price of a Slave. Joseph was the son of Jacob by Rachel, the grandson of Isaac, and the great-grandson of Abraham, and was sold as a slave to some Midianite merchants for a mere 20 pieces of silver by his jealous brothers in about 1750 B.C.E. (Genesis 37:28; 42:21) Throughout the stream of time, we find inflation in the slave trade, and the Biblical account of the price for Joseph falls exactly where it should to be in harmony with secular archaeology, as you can see in chart 1. Again, our alleged "J," "E," "D," and "P" composers would be a thousand years removed from Abraham, and "R" (the redactor) even further; thus they would have no access to this information so as to have gotten it correct. Only the actual writer, Moses, would be aware of this information by family records or oral tradition.

The Inflation of the Slave Trade in Biblical Times (Wood, 1996)

Source	Date	Price of a Slave in Silver
Akkad and 3rd Ur Dynasties	2000 B.C.E.	8–10 pieces of silver
Joseph (Genesis 37:2, 28)	1750 B.C.E.	20 pieces of silver

Hammurabi Code	1799–1700 B.C.E.	20 pieces of silver
Old Babylonian Tablets	B.C.E.	15–30 pieces of silver
Mari tablets	1799–1600 B.C.E.	20 pieces of silver
Exodus 21:32	1520–1470 B.C.E.	30 pieces of silver
Nuzi tablets	1499–1400 B.C.E.	30 pieces of silver
Ugarit tablets	1399–1200 B.C.E.	30–40 pieces of silver
Assyria	First-millennium B.C.E.	50–60 pieces of silver
2 Kings 15:20	790 B.C.E.	50 pieces of silver
Persia	750–500 B.C.E.	90–120 pieces of silver

Seti I began much like his father Ramses, as a military commander. His military prowess led to many triumphs that are recorded on the walls of the temple of Amon-Ra at Karnak. Here Seti I recorded his military triumphs; captives are shown being seized by their hair. As was expressed earlier, victories were proudly recorded on Egyptian monuments, but embarrassing or critical events were ignored, that is, never chiseled into their annals of history.

Concluding Thoughts

I had given much thought to a conclusion that contained quotations from many reputable scholars who use thought-provoking points to support the writership of Moses for the Pentateuch, but what would that prove? Certainly, if you quote a reputable scholar you would add weight to an argument, but it does not make the case. It only validates that you are not alone in your reasoning. Therefore, I have added quotations of only two scholars to make just that point. One does not count the number of people who believe one thing as opposed to another and those with the most votes win. No, the results should be based on evidence. In fact, the higher critics will infer that they are in the right by saying, 'Today, you will hardly find one scholar in the world who will argue for the writership of Moses for the Pentateuch.' If that makes them in the right, it also makes them in the wrong. Why? Because for centuries, for millenniums, the majority of Bible scholars—in the Jewish world, the Christian world, and the Islamic world—accepted Moses' writership; that is, until the Age of Reason within the eighteenth and nineteenth centuries when people started to question not only the writership of Moses but the very existence of God.

Would any Christian living in 1700 C.E. have ever doubted the writership of Moses? Hardly! So how did the Documentary Hypothesis become Documentary Fact? All it took was for some leading professors at major universities to plant seeds of doubt within their students. Being at the entrance of the era of higher criticism and skepticism of the nineteenth century, this Documentary Hypothesis had a well-cultivated field in which to grow. It created a domino effect as a few scholars produced a generation of students, who would then be the next generation of scholars, and so on.

As we moved into the twentieth century, these questions had become "facts" in the eyes of many; in fact, it became in vogue to challenge the Bible. Leading schools and leading scholars of higher criticism were the norms, and soon the conservative Christian was isolated. The twentieth-century student received a lean diet from those few scholars who still accepted God's Word as just that, the Word of God, fully inerrant, with 40 writers of 66 books over a period of about 1,600 years. No, these students would now be fed mostly liberal theology, and any who disagreed were portrayed as ignorant and naïve. This planting of uncertainty or mistrust, with question after question bringing Moses' writership into doubt, with most literature focusing on this type of propaganda, would create the latest generation of scholars, and today they dominate the world of scholarship.

How did this progressive takeover come off without a hitch? The conservative scholarship of the early twentieth century saw these liberal naysayers as nothing more than a fly at a picnic. Most did not even deem it necessary to address their questions, so by 1950–1970, the Documentary Hypothesis machine was in full throttle. It was about this same time that the sleeping giant finally awoke to find that conservative scholarship had taken a backseat to this new creature, liberal scholarship. It is only within the last 30–40 years that some very influential conservative scholars have started to publish books in a move to dislodge this liberal movement.* Is it too little, too late?

> *This is not to say that the 19th and early 20th century did not have any apologist defending against biblical criticism. There were some giants in this field, like R. A. Torrey.

It is possible to displace higher criticism, but many factors stand in the way. For one, any opposition is painted as uninformed and inexperienced regarding the subject matter. Moreover, the books that tear down the Bible with all their alleged critical analysis sell far better than those do that encourage putting faith in God's Word. In addition, many conservative scholars tend to sit on the sideline and watch as a few leading scholars attempt to do the work of the many. In addition, there are liberal scholars continually putting out numerous articles and books, dominating the market. Unlike the conservative scholars in the first part of the twentieth century, these liberal scholars in the first part of the twenty-first century are not slowing down. Moreover, they have become more aggressive.

The book *Introduction to the Bible,* by John Laux, explains just what the Documentary Hypothesis would have meant for the Israelites if it were true:

> The Documentary Theory is built up on assertions which are either arbitrary or absolutely false. . . . If the extreme Documentary Theory were true, the Israelites would have been the victims of a clumsy deception when they permitted the heavy burden of the Law to be imposed upon them. It would have been the greatest hoax ever perpetrated in the history of the world.[63]

It goes much further than that; it would mean that the Son of God was either fooled by what these higher critics argue, that there was a tradition of Moses being the writer of the Pentateuch, which developed through time and was accepted as reality during Jesus' day, or that Jesus

---

63. John Laux, *Introduction to the Bible* (Chicago: Tan Books & Pub., 1992), 186.

was a liar, because he had lived in heaven prior to his coming down to earth and was aware of the deception but had continued a tradition that he knew to be false. The truth is that the Son of God was well aware that Moses was, in fact, the writer of the Pentateuch and he presented Moses as such because he was there at the time!

So again, because Jesus taught that Moses was, in fact, the writer of the Pentateuch, we have three options:

- Jesus knew Moses was the writer because Jesus was there, in heaven, prior to his Virgin birth and observed Moses as the writer; or
- Jesus knew that Moses was not the writer and simply perpetuated a Jewish tradition that Moses was the writer; or
- Jesus possessed a limited knowledge and simply believed something that was a tradition because he was unaware of it being such.

So, if Jesus knew Moses was *not* the writer and purposely conveyed misinformation for the sake of Jewish tradition, this makes Jesus a liar and therefore a sinner, which would contradict what Hebrews 4:15 says of him, that "he was without sin." If he was simply in ignorance and was mistakenly conveying misinformation, this certainly does away with Jesus having a prehuman existence. (John 1:1–2; 3:13; 6:38, 62; 8:23, 42, 58; Colossians 1:15–18; Revelation 3:14; Proverbs 8:22–30) Based on the scriptures and other evidence presented, we can conclude that Jesus was well aware that Moses was the writer, and that is what he truthfully taught.

Duane Garrett makes the following observation concerning the Documentary Hypothesis:

> The time has long passed for scholars of every theological persuasion to recognize that the Graf-Wellhausen theory, as a starting point

for continued research, is dead. The Documentary Hypothesis and the arguments that support it have been effectively demolished by scholars from many different theological perspectives and areas of expertise. Even so, the ghost of Wellhausen hovers over Old Testament studies and symposiums like a thick fog. . . . One wonders if we will ever return to the day when discussions of Genesis will not be stilted by interminable references to P and J. There are indications that such a day is coming. Many scholars are exploring the inadequacies of the Documentary Hypothesis and looking toward new models for explaining the Pentateuch.[64]

These world-renowned scholars who have gone left of center are witty and able to express thoughts, ideas, and feelings coherently, having conviction that leads unsuspecting ones who are not aware of the facts to accept ideas that are made to appear as smooth-fitting pieces in a large puzzle, thinking that they are nothing more than long-awaited answers. Sadly, many unsuspecting readers have taken their words as absolute truth.

Jesus quotes or alludes to 23 of the 39 books of the Hebrew Scriptures. Specifically, he quotes all five of the books attributed to Moses—the book of Deuteronomy 16 times alone, this obviously being one of his favorites. As we close this chapter, we are going to let our greatest witness take the stand. As you read Jesus' references to Moses and the Law you will undoubtedly notice that he viewed Moses' writership as historically true, completely authoritative, and inspired by God. If one does not accept,

---

[64] Garrett, Duane. Rethinking Genesis: The Sources and Authorship of the First Book of the Pentateuch (Grand Rapids: Baker Books, 1991), 13.

Moses, as the writer of the Pentateuch as Jesus did, is that not calling Jesus a liar.

As Christians, we accept what the Bible teaches as true. By way of common sense and sound reasoning, the vast majority of the issues of higher criticism's Social Progressive Christian and Christian Modernists have been answered quite easily by the conservative scholar in absolute terms: for example, F. David Farnell, Gleason L. Archer Jr., C. John Collins, K. A. Kitchen, Norman L. Geisler, and others. For the handful of issues left, we still have reasonable answers, which are not beyond a reasonable doubt at this time; we are quite content to wait until we are provided with the concrete answers that will make these few issues beyond all reasonable doubt. The last 150 years of evidence that has come in by way of archaeological discoveries, a better understanding of the original language, historical-cultural and contextual understanding, as well as manuscripts has answered almost all those doubtful areas that have been called into question by the higher critics. Therefore, because we lack the complete answers for a few remaining issues means nothing.

Consider this: A critic raises an issue, but it is answered by a new archaeological discovery a few years later. The critic runs to another issue, and it is later answered by an improved understanding of the original languages. Then he runs to look for yet another issue, and it is answered by thousands of manuscripts that are uncovered over a period of two decades. This has been the case with thousands of issues. What are we to think the agenda is of those who continue scouring God's Word looking for errors, discrepancies, and contradictions? How many times must they raise objections and be proven wrong before we stop listening to their cries? If that is the case, why do their books still outsell those that expose their erroneous thinking? Does that say something about the Christian community and their desire for tabloid scholarship (sensationalized stories)? Would the average Christian rather read an article or book by Dan Brown on how Jesus allegedly married and had sexual relations with Mary Magdalene and fathered children (false, of course), or read an article or book on the actual, even more fascinating account of Jesus' earthly life, based on the four Gospels?

For today's Christian, there is no more important study than the life and ministry of the real, historical Jesus Christ. The writer of the book of Hebrews exhorts us to **"fix our eyes on** Jesus," to **"consider him** who endured such opposition from sinful men." Moreover, Jehovah God himself commanded: "This is my Son, whom I love; with him I am well pleased. **Listen to him!**" (*NIV*, bolding added) While an apologetic of the study of the "*Historical Jesus*," or "*The Case for the Resurrection of Jesus*"[65] is certainly fine, the primary source of the four Gospels accounts of Matthew, Mark, Luke, and John should be first place, the starting point of any real investigation of Jesus' life and ministry. A life and ministry that viewed the Old Testament as historically true and of the greatest importance to his followers that he would leave behind after his ascension back to heaven.

We return to Wellhausen, who investigated his documentary hypothesis under the worldview of Israelite religion from an evolutionary model: (1) at the beginning it was animistic and spiritistic, (2) gradually developing into polytheism, (3) moving eventually into henotheism

---

65. **Recommended**: Gary R. Habermas, *The Historical Jesus: Ancient Evidence for the Life of Christ* (Joplin, MO: College Press, 1996); Gary R. Habermas, *The Case for the Resurrection of Jesus* (Grand Rapids, MI: Kregel, 2004); Craig A. Evans, *Fabricating Jesus: How Modern Scholars Distort the Gospels* (Downers Grove, IL: IVP Books, 2006); Timothy Paul Jones, *Misquoting Truth: A Guide to the Fallacies of Bart Ehrman's Misquoting Jesus* (Downers Grove, IL: IVP Books, 2007).

(choosing one god out of many), and finally (4) gravitating to monotheism. Wellhausen could not accept that this development took place in a short period but was an evolution that took more than a millennium. This evolutionary process is no longer held among today's critical scholarship.

Another obstacle was that Wellhausen did not believe in the miraculous and could not accept prophetic statements (for example, Genesis 49) happening before the actual events. This mindset was the catalyst behind his research.[66] Consequently, Wellhausen investigated the text with this way of thinking and that state of mind contributed to his discovering the Documentary Hypothesis issues of different uses of the divine name, discrepancies, repetitions (doublets), and differences in style and language, reading his views into the text (eisegesis).

The above facts of this book have easily demonstrated that the evidence of the documentary hypothesis is really no evidence at all. The modern-day critic has to deal with the lack of consensus on the part of his colleagues, who lack in agreement for the explanation of the sources.

> This failure to achieve consensus is represented by the occasional division of source strata into multiple layers (see Smend's J1 and J2) that often occasions the appearance of new sigla (for instance, Eissfeldt's L [*aienquelle*], Noth's G[*rundschrift*], Fohrer's N [for Nomadic], and Pfeiffer's S [for Seir]. A further indication of the collapse of the traditional documentary hypothesis is the widely expressed

---

[66] Tremper Longman III, and Raymond B. Dillard, *An Introduction to the Old Testament* (Grand Rapids: Zondervan, 2006), 43–44.

doubt that E was ever an independent source (Voz, Rudolph, Mowinckel; cf. Kaiser, IOT, 42 n. 18). Similar disagreements are also found in the dating of the sources. J has been dated to the period of Solomon by Von Rad, though Schmidt would argue for the seventh century, and Van Seters (1992, 34) has advocated an exile date. While most scholars believe P is postexilic, Haran has argued that it is to be associated with Hezekiah's reforms in the eighth century BC.[67]

While the lack of consensus is not in and of itself capable of disproving the proposition of sources other than Moses for the writing of the Pentateuch, it does cast even more doubt on the critical scholar's proposal that the new school of the Documentary Hypothesis has any more to offer than the old school of Wellhausen.

As this book has clearly demonstrated, Moses is the inspired author of the Pentateuch. At best, we can accept that it is likely that Joshua may have updated the text in Deuteronomy chapter 34, which speaks of Moses' death, and it is possible that Joshua may have made the reference in Numbers 12:3 that refer to Moses as being 'the humblest man on the face of the earth.'[68] In addition, we can accept that a later copyist [or even possibly Ezra, another inspired author] updated Genesis 11:28, 31 to read "of the Chaldeans," a name of a land and its inhabitants in the southern portion of Babylonia that *possibly* was not recognized as Chaldea until several hundred years after Moses.

> The origin of the Chaldeans is uncertain but may well be in the west, or else branches of the

---

67. Ibid., 49–50.

[68] For the possibility of Moses penning these words, see my comments in the first paragraph of section four.

family may have moved there (cf. Job 1:17). The general name for the area in the earliest period is unknown, since it was part of Sumer (*see* SHINAR); so it cannot be argued that the qualification of Abraham's home city UR as "of the Chaldeans" (Gen. 11:28, 31; 15:7; as later Neh. 9:7; cf. Acts 7:4) is necessarily a later insertion in the text.[69]

The same would hold true of a copyist updating Genesis 36:31, which reads: "Now these are the kings who reigned in the land of Edom before *any king reigned over the sons of Israel.*" Moses and Joshua were long gone for hundreds of years before Israel ever had a king over them.[70] The same would hold true again for Genesis 14:14, which reads: When Abram heard that his relative had been taken captive, he led out his trained men, born in his house, three hundred and eighteen, and went in pursuit *as far as Dan.* Dan was an area settled long after Moses death after the Israelites had conquered the Promised Land. This too is obviously an update as well, making it contemporary to its readers.[71]

---

[69] Geoffrey W. Bromiley, vol. 1, *The International Standard Bible Encyclopedia, Revised* (Wm. B. Eerdmans, 1988; 2002), 630.

[70] It should be noted that even this statement could belong to Moses, even though there were no kings in Israel at this time. How? He would be aware that Jehovah had promised Abraham that he would be so great that kings would come out of him (Gen 17:6) and the preparation for such is mentioned at Deuteronomy 17:14-20.

[71] It should be noted that this author does not accept higher criticisms unending desire to find source(s) for a book, because they have dissected it to no end. While there are a few details that may have been updated by a copyist, or even the inspired writer Ezra (writer of Chronicles and the book that bears his name), this does not mean that we accept the update, if it is such, as the inspired material that was originally written, unless it was done by another inspired writer like Joshua, Ezra, or Nehemiah, or even possibly Jeremiah. It is also possible that it could be an explanatory addition.

Reference to "Ur of the Chaldeans"[72] (11:28) identifies the native land of Haran but not necessarily of Terah and his sons Abram and Nahor. In fact, the inclusion of this information for Haran may suggest the ancestral home was elsewhere (for this discussion see comments on 12:1). "Ur of the Chaldeans" occurs three times in Genesis (11:28, 31; 15:7) and once elsewhere (Neh 9:7). Stephen identified the place of God's revelation to Abram as "Mesopotamia" from which he departed: "So he left the land of the Chaldeans and settled in Haran" (Acts 7:3–4). The "land [*chōra*] of the Chaldeans" rather than "Ur of the Chaldeans" is the Septuagint translation, as reflected in Stephen's sermon, which can be explained as either a textual slip due to the prior phrase "land of his birth" or the ancient translator's uncertainty about the identity of the site. J. W. Wevers proposes that due to the apposition of "land of his birth," the translator interpreted "Ur" as a region.[73, 74]

As we have already stated, the critic is fond of finding portions of the text that lack secular support and then summarily dismissing it as not being a real historical account. Once evidence surfaces to support their dismissal as being wrong and premature, they simply never mention this section again, but move on to another. The question that begs to be asked by the logical and reasonable mind

---

[72] Hb. "Chaldeans" כַּשְׂדִּים is *kaldu* (Akk.) in Assyrian texts, and the Gk. has καλδαιοι; the original *sd* has undergone a change to *ld* (see R. S. Hess, "Chaldea," *ABD* 1.886–87).

[73] J. W. Wevers, *Notes on the Greek Text of Genesis*, Septuagint and Cognate Studies 35 (Atlanta: Scholars Press, 1993), 158.

[74] K. A. Mathews, vol. 1B, *Genesis 11:27-50:26*, electronic ed., Logos Library System; The New American Commentary (Nashville: Broadman & Holman Publishers, 2007), 99–100.

is, how many times must this take place before they stop and accept the Bible as sound and reliable history? Let us look at the historicity of the above account of Abraham's men defeating the Mesopotamian kings, for it is historically sound. Information had become known in the 20th century that vindicates this account as being historically true, and removes yet another arguing point from those supporters of the documentary hypothesis:

> The name of Chedorlaomer, King of Elam, contains familiar Elamite components: *kudur* meant "servant," and *Lagamar* was a high goddess in the Elamite pantheon. Kitchen (Ancient Orient, p. 44) generally prefers the vocalization Kutir instead of Kudur and gives the references for at least three Elamite royal names of this type. He equates tidal with a Hittite name, Tudkhaliya, attested from the nineteenth century B.C. As for Arioch, one King of Larsa ("El-Larsa") from this era was Eri-aku ("Servant of the Moon-god"), whose name in Akkadian was *Arad-Sin* (with the same meaning). The Mari tablets refer to persons by the name of Ariyuk. The cuneiform of the original of Amraphel, formerly equated with Hammurabi of Babylon, is not demonstrable for the twentieth century (Hammurabi himself dates from the eighteenth century, but there may possibly be a connection with Amorite names like *Amud-pa-ila*, according to H. B. Huffman. . . . It should be added that according to G. Pettinato, the leading epigraphist of the Ebla documents dating from 2400–2250 B.C., mention is made in the Ebla tablets of Sodom (spelled *Si-da-mu*), Gomorrah (spelled in Sumerian cuneiform *I-ma-ar*), and Zoar (*Za-e-ar*). He feels that quite possibly these

may be the same cities mentioned in the Abrahamic narrative.[75]

W. F. Albright comments: In spite of our failure hitherto to fix the historical horizon of this chapter, we may be certain that its contents are very ancient. There are several words and expressions found nowhere else in the Bible and now known to belong to the second millenium. The names of the towns in Transjordania are also known to be very ancient.[76]

In the final analysis, based on both the internal and external evidence, we can absolute confidence that Moses was the author of the Pentateuch. The minor additions of Joshua, who was himself an inspired writer, as well as the handful of updates in the text to make it clearer to the then-current reader does no harm to the inspired message that God wished to convey.

---

75. Gleason L. Archer, *Encyclopedia of Bible Difficulties* (Grand Rapids: Zondervan, 1982), 90–91.

[76]. H. C. Alleman and E. E. Flack, *Old Testament Commentary* (Philadelphia: Fortress, 1954), 14.

Genesis 10:5, 20, and 31 Indicate That There Were Many Languages, while 11:1 Says "One Language." Why?

Genesis 10:5, 20, 31 Updated American Standard Version (UASV)

⁵ From these the coastland peoples spread in their lands, each with his own language, by their clans, in their nations. ²⁰ These are the sons of Ham, according to their families, their languages, their lands, and their nations. ³¹ These are the sons of Shem, according to their families, according to their languages, by their lands, according to their nations.

Genesis 11:1 Updated American Standard Version (UASV)

11 Now the whole earth had one language [literally, "one lip"] and the same words.

This is talking about two different time periods. In the earlier of the two, the tribes of Ham, Shem, and Japheth all spoke the same language. Later, the people rebelled against Jehovah's explicit command to spread out and fill the earth. (Gen. 9:1) Therefore, God confused their languages, to facilitate his purpose that they fill the earth. Now that they could no longer understand each other, they had no alternative but to spread out and fill the earth. It should be noted that each person did not receive a new language, each family did, which kept the families (tribes) together.

Linguistics has not shown us the origin of the Hebrew language. In fact, it has explained the root of any of the most ancient languages known, for example, Sumerian, Akkadian, Aramaean, and Egyptian.

The reason for this is because these languages have appeared already fully developed in the earliest written records that we have discovered. Therefore, the views of the different scholars about the roots of Hebrew, such as, that Hebrew derived from Aramaic or from some Canaanite dialect are speculative. The same would also apply to the source of any of the words in the Hebrew Scriptures, and those who have suggest Akkadian or Aramaic sources. Dr. Horowitz comments: "In the field of etymology there are wide differences of opinion among scholars, even among the very best of them." ... "And so we have these never ending differences between equally highly respected authorities."—Edward Horowitz, *How the Hebrew Language Grew* (Brooklyn, NY: KTAV Publishing House, 1993), xix, xx.

The Bible is the most trusted historical source, which gives us evidence of the origin or beginning of the Hebrew language. "In July 2008 Israeli archaeologist Yossi Garfinkel discovered a ceramic shard at Khirbet Qeiyafa **"Five lines of ancient script on a shard of pottery could be the oldest example of Hebrew writing ever discovered, an archaeologist in Israel says.** The shard was found by a teenage volunteer during a dig about 20km (12 miles) south-west of Jerusalem. Experts at Hebrew University said dating showed it was written 3,000 years ago – about 1,000 years earlier than the Dead Sea Scrolls. Lead archaeologist Yosef Garfinkel identified it as Hebrew because of a three-letter verb meaning 'to do' which he said was only used in Hebrew. 'That leads us to believe that this is Hebrew and that this is the oldest

Hebrew inscription that has been found'[77] Up until 2008, "the earliest Hebrew inscription thus far discovered, the Gezer Calendar, is from the tenth century B.C.E. and the Mesha Inscription from the ninth century B.C.E."[78]

Hebrew, of course, was spoken by "Abram the Hebrew" (Gen. 14:13), who was born around 2000 B.C.E., and his descendants. In turn, Abraham was a descendant of Noah's son Shem. (Ge 11:10-26) Hebrew is, of course, a Semitic language (Shem being the forerunner). It is true, not all of Shem's descendants continued to speak the "one language" (Gen. 11:1) that seems to predate the flood in its pure form. This is apparent from the differences that developed among the Semitic languages, which would include Hebrew, Aramaic, Akkadian, as well as the various Arabic dialects. Making some inferences here, we note that of the post-flood people living in the Mesopotamia area, it was Shem alone who received a blessing from God. (Gen. 9:26) Therefore, it is reasonable to believe that Shem did not have his language changed like the others who rebelled at the Tower of Babel. (Gen. 11:5-9) It only seems reasonable that Shem spoke the language of Hebrew and being that it was likely not changed, it was the same as it had been previously before the flood. In other words, it was the "one language" that had existed from Adam and thereafter, until the rebellion at Babel. (Gen. 11:1) Yes, we are inferring that the first language of man was what would later be called Hebrew. However, this does not mean that every language derived from and are related to the early Hebrew, as was said above every family and tribe except Shem had their language changed when they rebelled at Babel. What we are saying is, it seems likely

---

[77] "(Oldest Hebrew script' is found: BBC News. 30 October 2008. Retrieved 28 November 2018. http://tiny.cc/xoib1y)

[78] Susan Anne Groom, Linguistic Analysis of Biblical Hebrew (Carlisle, Cumbria; Waynesboro, GA: Paternoster Press, 2003), 8.

that Hebrew preceded all of the other languages, as secular history knows no other.

The Old Testament Text

The Old Testament, the inspired Word of God, how was it copied, maintained as to the textual reliability, and handed down throughout the past three thousand years?

It should be appreciated that what we possess today is nothing short of Word of God that the Old Testament writers penned throughout a 1,600-year period, from the time of Moses to Malachi. While it certainly is not provable that God personally preserved these documents by the same way that he miraculously inspired the Scriptures to be error-free; there is little doubt that he blessed the work of those who worked on the copies and has blessed our attempts at restoring the text. Skeptics would consider it as mere coincidence that, we have a storehouse of manuscript treasure for both the Old Testament and New Testament documents while secular writings are nowhere near so fortunate. The secular writings of antiquity are reflected in but a handful of manuscripts for any given author. Moreover, they are hundreds of years removed from the date of the original copy, making them less trustworthy; while the Old Testament and New Testament are preserved in tens of thousands of manuscripts, with a number being within a century or two from the original copy[79] (especially the NT).

---

[79] When we use the term "original" reading or "original" text in this publication, it is a reference to the exemplar manuscript by the New Testament author (e.g., Paul) and his secretary (e.g., Tertius) from which other copies was made for publication and distribution into the Christian communities. It should be noted that the author likely penned some books without the use of a secretary, such as the apostle John in First and Second John.

Isaiah 40:8 Updated American Standard Version (UASV)

> ⁸ The grass withers, the flower fades,
>   but the word of our God will stand forever.

The Bible reader has every right to ask if the book that he carries has been tainted throughout the centuries of copying and recopying. What we possess today, is it a complete reflection of what was penned so many centuries ago? Does the evidence suggest that the manuscripts have been transmitted faithfully from the original-language texts so that the reader of God's Word can feel safe that the Bible is trustworthy? We know that scribal errors have crept into the text, after centuries of copying by hand, but have the textual scholars been able to ascertain what the original text was? There are many excellent books that cover the trustworthiness of the text of the Old and New Testaments; we will not be able to go into in great detail herein, because of limited space, but we can lay an excellent foundation, and suggest further reading. However, what is covered will be very informative and beneficial to examine.[80]

Men that were chosen by God penned the original manuscripts in Hebrew and a very small portion in Aramaic languages. Moses was the first in the late 16th-century B.C.E.,[81] who wrote the first five books of the Bible, down to about 443 B.C.E., with Malachi penning the book that bears his name, and Nehemiah writing the book that bears his name, totaling 39 canonical books for

---

[80] **THE TEXT OF THE NEW TESTAMENT: The Science and Art of Textual Criticism by** Don Wilkins and Edward D. Andrews, ISBN-13: 978-1-945757-44-0

[81] B.C.E. means "before the Common Era," which is more accurate than B.C. ("before Christ"). C.E. denotes "Common Era," often called A.D., for *anno Domini,* meaning "in the year of our Lord."

the Hebrew Old Testament. There are no original manuscripts in existence today. Around 642 B.C.E., in the time of King Josiah, Hilkiah, the high priest "found the Book of the Law" of Moses, very likely the original copy, which had been stored away in the house of God. At this point, it had survived for some 871 years. Jeremiah was so moved by the particular discovery that he wrote about the occasion at 2 Kings 22:8-10. About 180 years later, in 460 B.C.E., Ezra wrote about the same incident as well. (2 Chron. 34:14-18) Ezra was very interested in this, not only because of the importance of the event itself but he "was a skilled scribe in the Law of Moses, which Jehovah, the God of Israel, had given." (Ezra 7:6, UASV) Considering Ezra's position, the fact he was a historian, a scribe, he would have had access to all of the scrolls of the Old Testament that had been copied and handed down up to his time. In some cases, some were likely the inspired originals from the authors themselves. It would seem that Ezra was well qualified to be the custodian of the manuscripts in his day.–Nehemiah 8:1-2

Period of Manuscript Copying

In the days of Ezra and beyond, there would have been an increasing need for copying the Old Testament manuscripts. As you may recall from your personal Bible study, the Babylonians took the Jews into captivity for seventy years. Most of the Jews did not return upon their release in 537 B.C.E., and after that. Tens of thousands stayed in Babylon while others migrated throughout the ancient world, settling in the commercial centers. However, the Jews would pilgrimage back to Jerusalem several times each year, for religious festivals. Once there, they would be reading from the Hebrew Old Testament and sharing in the worship of God. Over a century later in Ezra's day, the need to travel back to Jerusalem was no longer a concern, as they carried on their studies in places of worship known as synagogues, where they read aloud from the Hebrew Scriptures and discussed their meaning. As one might imagine, the scattered Jewish populations throughout the ancient world would have been in need of their own personal copies of the Hebrew Scriptures.

Within the synagogues, there was a storage room, known as the Genizah.[82] Over time, manuscripts would wear out to the point of tearing. Thus, it would have been placed in the Genizah and replaced with new copies. Before long, after the old manuscripts were built up in the Genizah, they would eventually need to be buried in the earth. They performed this duty, as opposed to just burning them, so the holy name of God, Jehovah (or Yahweh), would not be desecrated. Throughout many centuries, many thousands of Hebrew manuscripts were disposed of in this way. Gratefully, the well-stocked Genizah of the synagogue in Old Cairo was saved from this handling of their manuscripts, perhaps because it was enclosed and overlooked until the middle of the 19th century. In 1890, as soon as the synagogue was being restored, the contents of the Genizah were checked, and its materials were gradually either sold or donated. From this source, manuscripts that were almost complete and thousands of fragments have found their way to Cambridge University Library and other libraries in Europe and America.

Throughout the world, scholars have counted and cataloged about 6,300 manuscripts of all or portions of the Hebrew Old Testament. Textual scholars of the Hebrew Scriptures, for the longest time, had to be content with Hebrew manuscripts that only went back to the tenth

---

[82] The Genizah was storehouse for Hebrew books: a repository for Hebrew documents and sacred books that were no longer in use, e.g. because they are old and worn, but must not be destroyed.

century C.E. This, of course, meant that the Hebrew Old Testament was about 1,400 hundred years removed from the last book that had been penned. This, then, always left the question of the trustworthiness of those copies. However, all of that changed in 1947, in the area of the Dead Sea, there was discovered a scroll of the book of Isaiah. In following years more of these precious scrolls of the Hebrew Scriptures were found as caves in the Dead Sea area yielded an enormous amount of manuscripts that had been concealed for almost 1,900 years. Specialists in the area of paleography[83] have now dated some of these as far back as the third and second century B.C.E. The Dead Sea Scrolls as they have become known, vindicated the trust that had been placed in the Masoretic texts[84] that we have possessed all along. A comparative study of the approximately 6,000 manuscripts of the Hebrew Scriptures gives a sound basis for establishing the Hebrew text and reveals faithfulness in the transmission of the text.

The Hebrew Language

Hebrew is the language in which the thirty-nine inspired books of the Old Testament were penned, apart from the Aramaic sections in Ezra 4:8–6:18; 7:12–26; Dan. 2:4b–7:28; Jer. 10:11, as well as a few other words and phrases from Aramaic and other languages. The language is not called "Hebrew" in the Old Testament. At Isaiah 19:18 it is spoken of as "the language [Literally "lip"] of Canaan." The language that became known as "Hebrew" is first shown in the introduction to Ecclesiasticus, an

---

[83] Paleography is the study of ancient writings: the study of ancient handwriting and manuscripts

[84] Hebrew Bible: the traditional text of the Hebrew Bible revised and annotated by Jewish scholars between the 6th and 10th centuries C.E.

Apocrypha[85] book. Moses, being raised in the household of Pharaoh, would have been given the wisdom of Egypt, as well as the Hebrew language of his ancestors. This would have made him the perfect person to look through any ancient Hebrew documents that may have been handed down to him, giving him the foundation for the book of Genesis.

Later, in the days of the Jewish kings, Hebrew came to be known as "Judean" (UASV) that is to say, the language of Judah (Neh. 13:24; Isa. 36:11; 2 Ki. 18:26, 28). As we enter the period of Jesus, the Jewish people spoke an expanded form of Hebrew, which would become Rabbinic Hebrew. Nevertheless, in the Greek New Testament, the language is referred to as the "Hebrew" language, not the Aramaic. (John 5:2; 19:13, 17; Acts 22:2; Rev. 9:11) Therefore, for more than 2,000 years, Biblical Hebrew served God's chosen people, as a means of communication.

However, once God chose to use a new spiritual Israel, made up of Jew and Gentile, there would be a difficulty within the line of communication as not all would be able to understand the Hebrew language. It became evident, 300 years before the rise of Christianity; there was a need for the Hebrew Scriptures to be a translation into the Greek language of the day, because of the Jewish diaspora who lived in Egypt. Down to our day, all or portions of the Bible have been translated into about 2,287 languages.

Even the Bible itself expresses the need for translating it into all languages. Paul, quoting Deuteronomy 32:43, says, "Rejoice, O Gentiles ["people of the nations"], with his people." And again, 'Praise the Lord, all you Gentiles,

---

[85] The Old Testament Apocrypha are unauthentic writings: writings or reports that are not regarded as authentic.

and let all the peoples extol him.'" (Rom 15:10) Moreover, all Christians are given what is known as the Great Commission, to "go therefore and make disciples of all nations." (Matt 28:19-20) In addition, Jesus stated, "this gospel of the kingdom will be proclaimed throughout the whole world as a testimony to all nations." (Matt 24:14) All of the above could never take place without translating the original language into the languages of the nations. What is more, ancient translations of the Bible that are extant (still in existence) in manuscript form have likewise aided in confirming the high degree of textual faithfulness of the Hebrew manuscripts.

Earliest Translated Versions

Versions are translations of the Bible from Hebrew, Aramaic, and Greek into other languages (or Hebrew into Greek). Translation work has made the Word of God accessible to billions of persons, who are incapable of understanding the original Biblical languages. The early versions of the Scriptures were handwritten and were, therefore, in the form of manuscripts. However, since the beginning of the printing press in 1455 C.E., many additional versions, or translations, have appeared, and these have been published in great quantities. Some versions have been prepared directly from Hebrew and Greek Bible texts, whereas others are based on earlier translations.

The Septuagint

The Septuagint is the common term for the Old Greek translation of the Hebrew Scriptures. The word means "seventy" and is frequently shortened by using the Roman numeral LXX, which is a reference to the tradition 72 Jewish translators (rounded off), who are alleged to have produced a version in the time of Ptolemy II Philadelphus (285-246 B.C.E.). The first five books of Moses being done around 280 B.C.E., with the rest being completed by 150 B.C.E. As a result, the name Septuagint came to denote the complete Hebrew Scriptures translated into Greek.

Acts 8:26-38 Updated American Standard Version (UASV)

Philip and the Ethiopian Eunuch

26 But an angel of the Lord spoke to Philip saying, "Get up and go south to the road that descends from Jerusalem to Gaza." (This is a desert road.) 27 And he rose and went. And there was an Ethiopian, a eunuch, a court official of Candace, queen of the Ethiopians, who was in charge of all her treasure; who had come to worship in Jerusalem, 28 and he was returning and sitting in his chariot, and was reading the prophet Isaiah. 29 And the Spirit said to Philip, "Go over and join this chariot." 30 So Philip ran to him and heard him reading Isaiah the prophet and asked, "Do you understand what you are reading?" 31 And he said, "How can I, unless someone guides me?" And he invited Philip to come up and sit with him. 32 Now the passage of the Scripture that he was reading was this:

"He was led as a sheep to slaughter
    and like a lamb before its shearer is silent,
    so he opens not his mouth.
33 In his humiliation was taken away.
    Who can describe his generation?
For his life is taken away from the earth."[86]

34 And the eunuch answered Philip and said, "I beg you, of whom does the prophet say this? Of himself or of someone else?" 35 Then Philip opened his mouth, and beginning from this Scripture he declared to him the good

---

[86] A quotation from Isaiah 53:7–8

news about Jesus. ³⁶ And as they went along the road they came to some water; and the eunuch said, "Look! Water! **What prevents me from being baptized?**"⁸⁷ ³⁸ And he commanded the chariot to stop, and they both went down into the water, Philip and the eunuch, **and he baptized him.**

The Eunuch court official was an influential man, who was in charge of the treasury of the queen of Ethiopia and to whom Philip preached. He was a proselyte [convert] to the Jewish religion who had come to Jerusalem to worship God. He had been reading aloud from the scroll of Isaiah (53:7-8 as our English Bible has it sectioned), and was puzzled as to who it was referring to; however, Philip explained the text, and the Eunuch was moved to the point of being baptized. The Eunuch was not reading from the Hebrew Old Testament; rather he was reading from the Greek translation, known as the Greek Septuagint. This work was very instrumental to both Jews and Christians in the Greek-speaking world in which they lived.

What contributed to the Hebrew Old Testament being translated into Greek and when and how did it occur? What was the need that brought the Septuagint about? How has it affected the Bible throughout these last 2,200 years? What impact does the Septuagint still have for the translator today?

---

⁸⁷ p⁴⁵, ⁷⁴ ℵ AB C 33 81 614 vg syr^(p, h) cop^(sa, bo) eth omit vs 37; E, many minuscules, it^(gig, h) vg^(mss) syr^(h with *) cop^(G67) arm, And Philip said, "If you believe with all your heart, you may." And he replied, "I believe that Jesus Christ is the Son of God."

The Greek-Speaking Jews and the Septuagint

In 332 B.C.E., Alexander the Great had just finished destroying the Phoenician city of Tyre, and was now entering Egypt, but was received as a great deliverer, not as a conqueror. It was here that he would found the city of Alexandria, bringing mankind one of the great learning centers of all time in the ancient world. The result of Alexander's conquering much of the then known world was the spread of Greek culture and the Greek language. Alexander himself spoke Attic Greek, which was the dialect that spread throughout the territories that he conquered. As the Attic dialect spread, it interacted with other Greek dialects, as well as the local languages, resulting in what we call Koine Greek or common Greek spreading throughout this vast realm.

Fragment of a Septuagint

By the time of the third century B.C.E., Alexandria had a large population of Jews. King Nebuchadnezzar of Babylon destroyed Jerusalem and exiled its people to Babylon centuries before. Many Jews had fled to Egypt at the time of the destruction. The returning Jews in 537, were scattered throughout southern Palestine, migrating to Alexandria after it was founded. The need for a Greek translation of the Hebrew Scriptures arose out of the necessity for the Jews in their worship services and education within the Jewish community of Alexandria.

Many of the Jews in Alexandria could no longer understand the Hebrew language, with others simply letting it grow out of practice. Most could only speak the common Greek of the Mediterranean world. However, they remained Jews in custom and culture and wanted to be able to understand the Scriptures that affected their everyday lives and worship. Therefore, the time was right for the production of the first translation of the Hebrew Scriptures.

Aristobulus of Paneas (c. 160 B.C.E.) wrote that the Hebrew law was translated into Greek, being completed during the reign of Ptolemy Philadelphus (285-246 B.C.E.). We cannot be certain as to what Aristobulus meant by the term "Hebrew law." Some have suggested that it encompassed only the Mosaic Law, the first five books of the Bible while others suggested that it was the entire Hebrew Scriptures.

Beginning of the Letter of Aristeas to Philocrates. Biblioteca Apostolica Vaticana, 11th century.

Letter of Aristeas

This Greek writing is allegedly a letter written by Aristeas, who was a high official in the court of Ptolemy II in Alexandria. It was sent to Jerusalem in order to secure a copy of the Jewish Law together with a group of seventy-two scholars who would translate the Law from Hebrew to Greek. The recipient is Philocrates, about whom nothing is said except that he was a brother of Aristeas. The alleged purpose of the book is to tell the story of the translation of the Septuagint.

The book contains a delightful story. Demetrius of Phalerum, head of the great library in Alexandria, suggests to the king that a translation be made of the Hebrew Law. The king writes to the high priest Eleazar in Jerusalem requesting him to send seventy-two scribes to perform the work of translation. He sends rich gifts for the temple in Jerusalem. The story includes a description of the Holy City. Eleazar delivers an apologetic for the Law. When the translators come to Alexandria, they are feted in a series of royal banquets. The king plies the scribes with philosophical questions, and they answer with amazing wisdom. Then they are taken to the island of Pharos in the harbor of Alexandria where they set to work. Demetrius compares their work every day and writes down a consensus. They complete the work in seventy-two days. It is then read to the Jews, who laud it. When it is read to the king, he is greatly impressed and expresses wonder as to why it has not been mentioned in earlier Greek literature. Demetrius says that earlier authors were divinely restrained from mentioning it. Finally, the translators are sent home bearing rich gifts.

It is obvious that this beautiful story is fictional, although it has a core of reliable information. Aristeas and Philocrates are not known in other historical literature. Furthermore, the Letter of Aristeas itself reflects the knowledge and usage of the LXX. The work also bears obvious unhistorical traits. For example, an Egyptian king would not attribute his throne to the Jewish God (37). The author, however, seems to be thoroughly familiar with the technical and official language of the court and of Alexandrian life and customs.

The purpose of the book is fairly obvious. It is a piece of Hellenistic Jewish apologetic writing designed to commend the Jewish religion and law to the Gentile world. The book emphasizes the honors showered on the seventy by the Greek king. High praise is accorded to Jewish wisdom by heathen philosophers. It explains the failure of Greek historians and poets to mention Jewish law. The apology of Eleazar on the inner meaning of the law tries to interpret in meaningful categories the Jewish distinction between clean and unclean things. The Jews are said to worship the same god as the Greeks but under a different name. Zeus is really the same as God (16).

The book is really not a true letter but belongs to the genre that may be called belles lettres. It falls in the Greek literary and artistic traditions rather than in the Semitic pattern. This governs its purpose, which is not to impart sound historical information but to produce a general ethical effect. The book is therefore far more important as a reflection of Jewish life and culture in the 2nd cent B.C. than as an account of the formation of the LXX. Thus very little attention is actually given to the work done on the LXX. We know that in the 2nd cent. B.C., before anti-Semitism had raised its head, a large colony of Jews lived in Alexandria, and the work reflects the fact that they were enthusiastically embracing Hellenistic culture, social usages, literary forms, and philosophical beliefs so far as they did not directly oppose their central religious tenets.

The date of the book is an almost insoluble problem. Scholars date it variously from 200 b.c. to 63 b.c. Perhaps an estimate of about 100 b.c. will suffice. While some scholars think that the LXX involved a protracted development, this letter may reflect the fact that at some time an official translation was made.[88]

---

[88] G. E. Ladd, "Pseudepigrapha," ed. Geoffrey W. Bromiley, *The International Standard Bible Encyclopedia, Revised* (Wm. B. Eerdmans, 1979–1988), 1041.

Useful in the First Century

The Septuagint was put to use at great length by Greek-speaking Jews both prior to and throughout first-century Christianity. Just after Jesus ascension, at Pentecost 33 C.E., almost a million Jews customarily gathered in Jerusalem for the Passover and Festival of Weeks, coming from such places as the districts of Asia, Egypt, Libya, Rome, and Crete, places that spoke Greek. There is little doubt that these were using the Septuagint in their services. (Acts 2:9-11) As a result, the Septuagint played a major role in spreading the Gospel message in the Jewish and proselyte communities. For example, we can look to Stephen.[89]

Acts 6:8-10 Updated American Standard Version (UASV)

8 And Stephen, full of grace and power, was performing great wonders and signs among the people. 9 But some men from what was called the Synagogue of the Freedmen, both Cyrenians and Alexandrians and some from Cilicia and Asia, rose up and disputed with Stephen. 10 But they were not able to withstand the wisdom and the Spirit with which he was speaking.

In his defense, Stephen gave a long history of the Israelite people, and at one point he said,

---

[89] "The first Christian martyr; foremost of those chosen to bring peace to the quarreling church (Acts 6:1–7) and so mighty in the Scriptures that his Jewish opponents in debate could not refute him (Acts 6:10) as he argued that Jesus was the Messiah. Saul of Tarsus heard Stephen's speech to the Jewish Sanhedrin accusing the Jewish leaders of rejecting God's way as their forefathers had (Acts 6:12–7:53). Saul held the clothes of those who stoned Stephen to death; he saw him die a victorious death." (Brand, Draper and Archie 2003, p. 1534)

Acts 7:12-14 Updated American Standard Version (UASV)

¹² But when Jacob heard that there was grain in Egypt, he sent our fathers the first time. ¹³ On the second visit Joseph made himself known to his brothers, and the family of Joseph became known to Pharaoh. ¹⁴ And Joseph sent and summoned Jacob his father and all his kindred, seventy-five persons in all.

This account comes from Genesis chapter 46, verse 27, which reads, "All the persons of the house of Jacob who came into Egypt were seventy." The Hebrew Old Testament reads seventy, but it is the Septuagint that reads seventy-five. Therefore, Stephen was referencing the Septuagint in his defense before the synagogue of the Freedmen.

The Apostle Paul traveled about 10,282 miles on his missionary tours,[90] which brought him into contact with Gentiles, who feared the God of the Bible and the devout Greeks who worshiped God. (Acts 13:16, 26; 17:4) These became worshipers or fearers of God because they had access to the Septuagint. The Apostle Paul used the Septuagint quite often in his ministry, and his letters.–Genesis 22:18; Galatians 3:8

The Greek New Testament contains about 320 direct quotations, as well as a combined 890 quotations and paraphrases from the Hebrew Old Testament. Most of these are from the Septuagint. Therefore, those Septuagint quotes and paraphrases became a part of the inspired Greek New Testament. Jesus had said, "you will be my witnesses in Jerusalem and in all Judea and Samaria, and to the end of the earth." (Acts 1:8) He had also foretold,

---

[90] Stanford University recently unveiled ORBIS, a site that lets you calculate the time and cost required to travel by road or ship around the Roman world in A.D. 200. (University 2012)

"this gospel of the kingdom will be proclaimed throughout the whole world." (Matt 24:14) For this to take place, it had to be translated into other languages, to reach the people earth wide.

Still Beneficial Today

The Septuagint's great purpose today is the light that it sheds on textual variants that crept into the Hebrew Old Testament text, as it was being copied throughout the centuries. An example of this can be found in Genesis 4:8, which reads,

Genesis 4:8 Updated American Standard Version (UASV)

8 Cain said to Abel his brother. "Let us go out into the field."[91] And it came about when they were in the field, that Cain rose up against Abel his brother and killed him.

The portion "let us go out to the field" is not in the tenth century C.E. Hebrew manuscripts. However, it is found in the earlier Septuagint manuscripts, as well as the Samaritan Pentateuch,[92] the Peshitta,[93] and the Vulgate.[94] **First**, the Hebrew that is used to introduce speech [*yomer*, "to say something"] is in the Hebrew text, "Cain Spoke." However, no speech follows in the Hebrew text. Many scholars argue that these words were in the original Hebrew text, but were omitted accidentally very early.

---

[91] **Genesis 4:8**: SP LXX It Syr inserts these bracketed words; Vg, "Let us go outdoors"; MT omits; some MSS and editions have an interval here.

[92] This version only encompasses the first five books, and is really a transliteration of the Hebrew text into Samaritan script, developed from the ancient Hebrew script.

[93] The Syriac version of the Bible, written around the 4th century.

[94] A Latin version of the Bible, produced by Saint Jerome in the 4th century.

Second, a few others, on the other hand, claim that the Hebrew that is used to introduce speech [*yomer*, "to say something"] is used in three other passages, with nothing being said. Therefore, they maintain that the more difficult and shorter reading is original, which would mean that the Greek translators added the words to complete the meaning. This book supports the first textual argument, along with the majority of scholars. Herein, we see how the Septuagint can help in identifying textual errors that may have crept into the Hebrew text over centuries of copying.

The text of the LXX is largely close to that of the Masoretes and Vulgate. For instance, Genesis 4:1-6 is identical in both the LXX, Vulgate and the Masoretic Text. Similarly, Genesis 4:8 to the end of the chapter is the same. There is only one visible difference in that chapter, at 4:7

Genesis 4:7, LXX and English Translation (NETS)	Genesis 4:7, Masoretic and English Translation from MT (Judaica Press)	Genesis 4:7, Latin Vulgate and English Translation (Douay-Rheims)
οὐκ ἐὰν ὀρθῶς προσενέγκῃς, ὀρθῶς δὲ μὴ διέλῃς, ἥμαρτες; ἡσύχασον· πρὸς σὲ ἡ ἀποστροφὴ αὐτοῦ, καὶ σὺ ἄρξεις αὐτοῦ.	הֲלוֹא אִם תֵּיטִיב שְׂאֵת וְאִם לֹא תֵיטִיב לַפֶּתַח חַטָּאת רֹבֵץ וְאֵלֶיךָ תְּשׁוּקָתוֹ וְאַתָּה תִּמְשָׁל בּוֹ:	nonne si bene egeris recipes sin autem male statim in foribus peccatum aderit sed sub te erit appetitus eius et tu dominaberis illius
If you offer correctly but do	Is it not so that if you improve,	If thou do well, shalt thou not

not divide correctly, have you not sinned? Be still; his recourse is to you, and you will rule over him.	it will be forgiven you? If you do not improve, however, at the entrance, sin is lying, and to you is its longing, but you can rule over it.	receive? but if ill, shall not sin forthwith be present at the door? but the lust thereof shall be under thee, and thou shalt have dominion over it.

However, the Hebrew text is the foundation and most trustworthy text. Thus, it is used to correct the Septuagint text as well. It is by the comparison of the Hebrew manuscripts, and the many early versions that we discover any textual errors, and establish the original reading. This can give us confidence that we are reading the Word of God. Old Testament textual scholar, Paul D. Wegner writes,

> The job of the textual critic is very similar to that of a detective searching for clues as to the original reading of the text. It is reminiscent of the master detective Sherlock Holmes who could determine a number of characteristics of the suspect from the slightest of clues left at the crime scene. In our case the "crime scene" is the biblical text, and often we have far fewer clues to work from than we would like. Yet the job of the textual critic is extremely important, for we are trying to determine the exact reading of a text in

order to know what God has said and expects from us.[95]

We have complete copies of the Septuagint that go back to the fourth century C.E., and many other fragments that date much earlier. Some of these **do contain** the divine name, Jehovah (JHVH/YHWH). This is represented in the Hebrew text with what is known as the Tetragrammaton.[96] What these copyists have done is to substitute the divine name or Tetragrammaton with the Greek words for "God" and "Lord." However, with the discovery of the Dead Sea Scrolls, were the discovery of a leather fragment scroll that contained the minor prophets (Hosea through Malachi), written in Greek. These have been dated to the time between 50 B.C.E. and 50 C.E. In these Greek Old Testament texts were the Tetragrammaton. Thus, in the earlier Septuagint version, they retained the divine name.

(יהוה) (1) LXX[P. Fouad Inv. 266] renders the divine name by the Tetragrammaton written in square Hebrew characters in the following places: De 18:5, 5, 7, 15, 16; 19:8, 14; 20:4, 13, 18; 21:1, 8; 23:5; 24:4, 9; 25:15, 16; 26:2, 7, 8, 14; 27:2, 3, 7, 10, 15; 28:1, 1, 7, 8, 9, 13, 61, 62, 64, 65; 29:4, 10, 20, 29; 30:9, 20; 31:3, 26, 27, 29; 32:3, 6, 19. **(first century B.C.E.)**

---

[95] Paul D. Wegner, A Student's Guide to Textual Criticism of the Bible: Its History, Methods & Results (Downers Grove, Ill.: InterVarsity Press, 2006), 22-23.

[96] **Hebrew name for God:** a four-letter Hebrew name for God revealed to Moses, usually written JHVH or YHWH (Exodus 3:13-14). Judaism of Jesus' day, in their traditions, regarded this name as too sacred to be pronounced. Jesus said of such traditions, "thus making void the word of God by your tradition that you have handed down." (Mark 7:13)

(𐤉𐤄𐤅𐤄)   (2) LXX^(VTS 10a) renders the divine name by the Tetragrammaton written in ancient Hebrew characters in the following places: Jon 4:2; Mic 1:1, 3; 4:4, 5, 7; 5:4, 4; Hab 2:14, 16, 20; 3:9; Zep 1:3, 14; 2:10; Zec 1:3, 3, 4; 3:5, 6, 7. (end of the first century C.E.)

(3) LXX^(IEJ 12) renders the divine name by the Tetragrammaton written in ancient Hebrew characters in Jon 3:3. (end of the first century C.E.)

(𐤉𐤄𐤅𐤄)   (4) LXX^(VTS 10b) renders the divine name by the Tetragrammaton written in ancient Hebrew characters in the following places: Zec 8:20; 9:1, 1, 4. (middle of the first century C.E.)

IAω (IAO)   (5) 4Q LXX Lev^b renders the divine name in Greek letters ? (*IAO*) in Le 3:12; 4:27. (first century B.C.E.)

(𐤉𐤉)   (6) LXX^(P. Oxy. VII.1007) renders the divine name by abbreviating the Tetragrammaton in the form of a double *Yohdh* in Ge 2:8, 18. (third century C.E.)

(יהוה)   (7) Aq^Burkitt renders the divine name by the Tetragrammaton written in ancient Hebrew characters in the following places: 1Ki 20:13, 13, 14; 2Ki 23:12, 16, 21, 23, 25, 26, 27. (end of the fifth century or the beginning of the sixth century C.E.)

(יהוה)   (8) Aq^Taylor renders the divine name by the Tetragrammaton written in ancient Hebrew characters (??) in the following places: Ps 91:2, 9; 92:1, 4, 5, 8, 9;

96:7, 7, 8, 9, 10, 13; 97:1, 5, 9, 10, 12; 102:15, 16, 19, 21; 103:1, 2, 6, 8. (**after the middle of the fifth century C.E., but not later than the beginning of the sixth century C.E.**)

(𐤉𐤄𐤅𐤄 or 𐤉𐤄𐤅𐤄) (9) Sym[P. Vindob. G. 39777] renders the divine name by the Tetragrammaton written in archaic Hebrew characters in the following places: Ps 69:13, 30, 31. (**fourth century C.E.**)

(ΠΙΠΙ) (10) Ambrosian O 39 sup. renders the divine name by the Tetragrammaton written in square Hebrew characters (??) in all five columns in the following places: Ps 18:30, 31, 41, 46; 28:6, 7, 8; 29:1, 1, 2, 2, 3, 3; 30:1, 2, 4, 7, 8, 10, 10, 12; 31:1, 5, 6, 9, 21, 23, 23, 24; 32:10, 11; 35:1, 22, 24, 27; 36:Sup, 5; 46:7, 8, 11; 89:49 (in columns 1, 2 and 4), 51, 52. (**end of the ninth century C.E.**)

The year 1971 brought us the release for publication of Papyrus Fouad 266, which is a copy of the Pentateuch in the Greek version of the Hebrew Bible, also a Septuagint version. It is a papyrus manuscript in scroll form. The manuscript has been assigned palaeographically to the second or first century B.C.E. The manuscript has survived in a fragmentary condition. The divine name is preserved here as well.

The Aramaic Targums

The Aramaic word for "interpretation" or "paraphrase" is *targum*. (Brand, Draper and Archie 2003, p. 1558) After the exile from Babylon in 539 B.C.E., the Jews living in the territory of the Persian Empire came to use the common language of Aramaic. Therefore, it became necessary to have a translation of the Hebrew Old Testament in the Aramaic language. They probably assumed their current form by about the fifth century C.E. Although they are simply free paraphrases of the Hebrew text and not an accurate translation, they are a source of rich background to the text and give assistance in determining some problematic passages. In addition, "the material is of interest to NT scholars who attempt to understand the Judaism of which Jesus was a part." (IBID,. 1558) Paul D. Wegner writes,

> Following the return from exile in 538 b.c., the Jewish people primarily spoke Aramaic (Neh 8:7–8; 13:24) and grew increasingly less familiar with Hebrew. As a result, the Scripture lessons needed to be translated into Aramaic and became known as Targums. Some Targums contain a literal translation of the Hebrew text (e.g., Targum Onkelos), whereas others are paraphrastic (adding interpretive and explanatory material; e.g., Targum Neofiti).[97] Philip S. Alexander explains how these more paraphrastic translations arose: "It came to be recognized, however, that the Targum could do more than provide a simple rendering of Scripture into everyday speech: it could be a commentary as well as a translation, and impose a comprehensive interpretation on the original Hebrew."[98] At first these explanations were given extemporaneously by the scribes and teachers, it being strictly forbidden to put them into writing; thus various oral versions existed simultaneously.[99] It later became

---

[97] For a good example of this see Brad H. Young, "Targum," *ISBE* 4:727–28.

[98] Philip S. Alexander, "Targum, Targumim," *ABD* 6:321.

[99] Johannes C. de Moor, "Systems of Writing and Nonbiblical Languages," in *Bible Handbook,* vol. 1, *The World of the Bible,* ed. Adam S. van der Woude, trans. Sierd Woudstra (Grand Rapids: Eerdmans, 1986), p. 116. Würthwein suggests that the Aramaic translation was to be given orally in the worship service to separate it from the sacred text (*Text of the Old Testament,* p. 75). See also Gamaliel I (mid-first century

obvious that to standardize these translations, they would have to be written. There are targums for every book of the Hebrew Bible except Ezra-Nehemiah and Daniel; two targums were even found at Qumran (11QtgJob; 4QtgLev).[100]

The interpretive element in the targums is clear; scribes tended to paraphrase, use explanatory phrases and reinterpret the text in order to better convey its meaning. There were two primary schools of textual study: a western school centered in Palestine at Tiberias, which existed until the end of the third century a.d. and then again from the eighth to tenth centuries a.d.; and an eastern school centered in Babylonia at Sura, Nehardea (destroyed in a.d. 259), and later at Pumbeditha.[101] Unlike the Palestinian school, the Babylonian school finally produced an official version of the targum about the fifth century A.D., but it gradually lost its influence and by the tenth or eleventh century A.D. had disappeared. Fragments of seven manuscripts of the Palestinian Targum, dating from the seventh to the ninth centuries A.D., have been found in the Cairo Genizah and greatly add to our knowledge of this targum.[102] Today only a fraction of these written Aramaic targums have survived; the major ones are listed below according to the biblical books.

---

a.d.) who was not willing to recognize a targum of Job (*Shabbat* 115a; cf. *Tosefta Shabbat* 13, 2).

[100] On 11QtgJob see Johannes P. M. van der Ploeg and Adam S. van der Woude, *Le targum de Job de la grotte XI de Qumran* (Leiden: Brill, 1971); Michael Sokoloff, *The Targum to Job from Qumran Cave XI*, Bar-Ilan Studies in Near Eastern Languages and Culture (Ramat Gan: Bar-Ilan University, 1974). On 4QtgLev see József T. Milik, in Roland de Vaux and József T. Milik, *Qumrân Grotte 4. II*, DJD 6 (Oxford: Clarendon, 1977), pp. 86–89.

[101] Würthwein, *Text of the Old Testament*, p. 14.

[102] Kahle, *Masoreten des Westens*, 2:1–65.

6.2.2.1 Pentateuch. There are more known targums for the Pentateuch than for any other part of the Old Testament, probably because of its importance the Jewish people. Since at least the Middle Ages, Targum Onkelos has been the official Babylonian targum of the Pentateuch and has been widely accepted by the Jews as the most authoritative targum for the Pentateuch.[103]

- *Neofiti I* (Biblioteka Apostolica Vaticana, Codex Neofiti I). This targum has been in the Vatican Library since 1956 when it was given to the library as part of a collection from the Pia Domus Neophytorum in Rome. A colophon dates this manuscript to a.d. 1504, but the text that is copied may be as old as the third to fourth centuries A.D. Neofiti I is a nearly complete Palestinian targum (missing only thirty verses for various reasons); the main text appears to have been written by three different scribes. It contains numerous glosses added in the margins or between the lines. Its translation is midway between the literalness of Targum Onkelos and the paraphrastic nature of Targum Jerusalem I.

- *Targum Jerusalem I* (sometimes erroneously called Pseudo-Jonathan). This targum is represented by two manuscripts: *editio princeps* prepared by Asher Forins, from Venice, in 1591 and the British Museum Ms. Add. 27031. Its present form dates to seventh to eighth centuries A.D. Targum Jerusalem I combines the official Targum Onkelos with much more material so that it is almost twice as long as the MT. This other material appears to come from a variety of sources, including the Palestinian Targum and other later rabbinic sources.

- *Targum Onkelos.* This targum is represented by several manuscripts housed at the Jewish Theological Seminary of America (Mss. 131, 133a, 152, 153) and Ms.

---

[103] Alexander, "Targum, Targumim," 6:321.

Ebr.[104] 448 at the Vatican Library. It is generally dated between the second to the fifth centuries A.D. and is also the most literal of the targums.

• *Fragment Targum* (Targum Jerusalem II). This targum is represented by Ebr.[105] 440, Biblioteca Apostolica Vaticana; MS Hébr. 110, Bibliothèque Nationale, Paris; etc. It is dated to the seventh to the fifteenth centuries a.d. (somewhere between Neofiti and Jerusalem Targum I). Little of this work remains, but it appears to contain midrashic material from the Palestinian Targum.

• *Cairo Genizah Mss.* These include at least nine fragmentary manuscripts of Targums for the Pentateuch. They are dated anywhere from the eighth to fourteenth centuries A.D. Some of these fragments contain the full Hebrew verse, while others include only *lemmata* (i.e., the opening words of a verse). For the most part they represent the Palestinian targum, though they are not always in agreement in places where they overlap.

• *Toseftot.* Some manuscripts that contain Toseftot (or additions) are Ms. Parva 3218; Ms. Sasson 282; Ms. Heb. e. 74 (Oxford); and Ms. T-S NS 184.81 (Cambridge). The date of these additions is uncertain. Some of the manuscripts of Targum Onkelos have additional haggadic materials (rabbinic statements that illustrate the Torah) that are labeled "Tosefta Yerushalmi."

6.2.2.2 Prophets. Targum Jonathan was the official Babylonian targum of the Prophets and was probably translated by Rabbi Joseph ben Ḥayya (c. A.D. 270–333), head of the academy of Pumbeditha (b. *B. Bat.* 3b; *Yoma* 32b).

---

[104] Hebrew

[105] Hebrew

- *Targum Jonathan.* This targum is dated from the fourth to fifth centuries a.d. and is represented by several Yemenite manuscripts with supralinear pointing (Ms. 229 Jewish Theological Seminary of America; Mss. Or. 2210 and 2211 British Museum) and Western Ms. with Tiberian pointing (Codex Reuchlinianus). The official Babylonian Targum of the Prophets was probably translated by Rabbi Joseph ben Ḥayya (c. A.D. 270–333), head of the academy of Pumbeditha (b. *B. Bat.* 3b; *Yoma* 32b). It bears many similarities to Targum Onkelos; though not generally expansive, it includes a significant amount of *Haggadah.*

- *Toseftot.* The additions to Targum Jonathan are written in the margins or in the text itself. They may be remnants of the Palestinian Targum of the Prophets that were retained by scribes when the Babylonian Talmud began to predominate the West. About eighty additions appear in the Codex Reuchlinianus though their date is uncertain.

6.2.2.3 Writings. There is no official targum for the Writings, but the medieval writers usually quote from Targum Yerushalmi (= Jerusalem) for these books.

- *Targum Yerushalmi (= Jerusalem).* The date is uncertain. This targum for each of the books is very different and often appears in more than one recension.

Technically the targums are not translations or paraphrases but commentaries on the biblical books; most can be dated no earlier than the fifth century A.D.

Mss. manuscripts

Or. Oriental (Eastern)

b. Babylonian Talmud

B. Bat. Baba Batra

Nevertheless they are important to textual criticism for several reasons: (1) they may contain early traditions concerning the reading of the text; (2) they include early Jewish traditions as to the interpretation of the biblical texts; and (3) they are written in Aramaic, which is closely related to biblical Hebrew. The quality of the translation varies greatly among the targums, but on the whole they reflect the proto-MT (except a Targum of Job found at Qumran). The Palestinian targums are generally more paraphrastic in nature than the Babylonian targums, with the exception of the two Palestinian targums found at Qumran, which are quite literal.[106]

The Latin Vulgate

This version has been the primary text used by many of the Catholic translators in turning out other versions in the many languages of Western Christianity. How did the Vulgate come about? The Latin word *vulgatus* means "common, that which is popular." Latin was once the official language of the Roman Empire. Even though Greek was the common language that most people spoke up until the fourth century C.E., there was still a need for Latin translations of the New Testament, which were produced in the second century, and are known as the Old Latin texts. However, as times passed, especially after Constantine the Great legalized Christianity in 313 C.E., the differences in the Old Latin texts eventually became unbearable.

When the Latin Vulgate was first produced, it was in the common, or popular, Latin of the day, which would have been understood without difficulty by the average

---

[106] Paul D. Wegner, *A Student's Guide to Textual Criticism of the Bible: Its History, Methods & Results* (Downers Grove, IL: InterVarsity Press, 2006), 172–175.

people of the Western Roman Empire. In 382 C.E., Pope Damasus commissioned the leading Bible scholar of the time, Jerome, his advisor, to revise the Old Latin text. Jerome made two revisions of the Old Latin Psalms, in comparison with the Greek Septuagint. His translation of the Vulgate Bible was made directly from the original Hebrew language of the Old Testament and Greek language of the New Testament and was, therefore, not a version of a version. This approach created great controversy at the time. Jerome worked on his Latin translation from the Hebrew from about 390 to 405 C.E. The completed work included apocryphal books, which were also in copies of the Septuagint by this time. However, Jerome plainly distinguished between the books that were canonical and those that were not. There are no less than 10,000 Latin manuscripts today, as well as 9,300 other early versions. Paul D. Wegner writes,

> The Latin Vulgate is very important to the study of the history of the Bible on two counts: (1) it held a dominant role in Western Europe for about one thousand years, and (2) during the Reformation, when people needed the Bible in their mother tongue, the Latin Vulgate was translated into many other languages. The Latin Vulgate was translated by Jerome during the years a.d. 383 to about 405. Pope Damasus I, bishop of Rome from about a.d. 366 to 384, commissioned Jerome (Sophronius Eusebius Hieronymus, c. a.d. 345–420), his secretary, to revise and standardize the Old Latin version. There were so many differences among Old Latin texts in circulation within the Latin church that people could not be certain which text to follow. Jerome himself commented on the great diversity of manuscripts, saying that there were "almost as many forms of text as there are manuscripts."[107]

---

[107] Metzger, *Bible in Translation*, p. 32. Schaff, *Nicene and Post-Nicene Fathers*, 6:487–88.

Jerome, a brilliant scholar with a firm grasp of Latin, Greek and later at least some knowledge of Hebrew, was called on to rectify this problem. He considered refusing the task, knowing that people would castigate him for changing the beloved wording of the Old Latin texts, and wrote to Pope Damasus the following:

> Is there anyone learned or unlearned, who, when he takes the volume in his hands and perceives that what he reads does not suit his settled tastes, will not break out immediately into violent language and call me a forger and profane person for having the audacity to add anything to the ancient books, or to make any changes or corrections in them?[108]

However, he later accepted the commission by the pope to undertake this important task.

His work, later known as the Latin Vulgate (*vulgate* means "common" or "plain" tongue), became the standard edition of the Bible for over one thousand years. His most important contribution was probably the Latin version of the Old Testament (390–405), which he translated from the original Hebrew text, being the only one in the Western church qualified to make such a translation.[109] He worked hard to learn Hebrew; even though his proficiency was limited, it was better than any other church father at the time. By the eighth or ninth century a.d., the Latin Vulgate had finally superseded the Old Latin version. The climax of its victory was on April 8,

---

[108] Schaff, *Nicene and Post-Nicene Fathers*, 6:487–88.

[109] Würthwein, *Text of the Old Testament*, p. 92. See also James Barr, "St. Jerome's Appreciation of Hebrew," *BJRL* 49 (1966/1967): 281–302.

1546, when the Council of Trent declared the Vulgate to be the authentic Bible of the Roman Catholic Church:

> But if any one receive not, as sacred and canonical, the said books entire with all their parts, as they have been used to be read in the Catholic Church, and as they are contained in the old Latin vulgate edition; and knowingly and deliberately contemn [condemn] the traditions aforesaid; let him be anathema (fourth session).[110]

In general, Jerome chose to translate his new work in a sense-for-sense rather than literal method.[111] He explained his procedure in a letter to the pope and claimed that he only changed the Old Latin text when it seemed absolutely necessary, and retained phrases in other cases that had become familiar to the people.[112] The text of the Vulgate is not uniform—either Jerome initially relied too heavily on the Old Latin manuscripts or perhaps he became a better translator with practice. This lack of uniformity may also indicate that Jerome was not able to translate the entire Bible; some have gone so far as to question whether he actually translated a good part of the New Testament (e.g., Pauline and Catholic Epistles, Acts and Revelation).[113] Nonetheless, Jerome used the Hebrew text as the basis for his translation of the Old Testament, which was a vast improvement. But he was severely criticized for this by the church, which claimed that the LXX

---

[110] Philip Schaff, *The Creeds of Christendom with a History and Critical Notes* (New York: Harper & Brothers, 1882), 2:82.

[111] Hendly D. F. Sparks, "Jerome as Biblical Translator," in *CHB* 1:523.

[112] Metzger, *Bible in Translation*, p. 33.

[113] Pierre-Maurice Bogaert, "Versions, Ancient (Latin)," *ABD* 6:801.

was inspired and therefore authoritative.[114] Some of Jerome's severest challenges came from those who wanted to include the Apocrypha; even Augustine disagreed with Jerome's Hebrew canon. The Apocrypha was finally included in the Vulgate, though Jerome did not spend much time on it. (Jerome left some apocryphal books untranslated from the Old Latin.)[115]

Because the Old Testament of the Latin Vulgate was translated directly from a Hebrew text, it may provide insight into the text at that time. Jerome's commentaries on the Minor Prophets, Isaiah, and Jeremiah (A.D. 406–420) are important to the history of Old Testament exegesis, showing how he interpreted the texts later. These commentaries demonstrate that Jerome used a variety of texts according to the reading that best fit his exegesis of the passage. In the New Testament, it is more difficult to determine the value of the Latin Vulgate to textual criticism, since the Old Latin texts significantly influenced parts of the translation, especially in the Gospels. In some passages, however, the Greek text underlying the translation may precede the Byzantine text type and thus provide some very early readings of the text.[116]

The Hebrew Texts

---

[114] Augustine, who represented a majority of people at the time, claimed that the lxx was inspired (*De Civitate Dei* 18.43), but Jerome questioned its inspiration (*Praefatio in Pentateuchum*, in *Biblia Sacra Iuxta Latinam Vulgatam Versionem*, ed. Francis Aidan Gasquet [Rome: Typis Polyglottis Vaticanis, 1926], 1:67; see also Werner Schwarz, *Principles and Problems of Biblical Translation* [Cambridge: Cambridge University Press, 1955], pp. 26–30).

[115] Metzger, *Bible in Translation*, p. 34.

[116] Paul D. Wegner, *A Student's Guide to Textual Criticism of the Bible: Its History, Methods & Results* (Downers Grove, IL: InterVarsity Press, 2006), 289–291.

The Sopherim

The Sopherim (scribes) were copyist from the days of Ezra down to the time of Jesus. While they were very serious about their task as a copyist, they did take liberties in making textual changes at times. Whether this was what Jesus had in mind cannot be know for certain, but Jesus condemned these scribes, for assuming powers that did not belong to them.–Matthew 23:2, 13.

"A note in the *Massorah* against several passages in the manuscripts of the Hebrew Bible states: '*This is one of the Eighteen Emendations of the Sopherim,*' or words of that effect." The intentions of these scribes were good, as they felt the passages were showing irreverence for God or one of his representatives here on earth. "These emendations were made at a period long before Christ before the Hebrew text had obtained its present settled form, and these emendations affect the Figure called *Anthropopatheia*."

"The following is a list of the eighteen 'Emendations,' together with eight others not included in the official lists. Particulars will be found on consulting the notes on the respective passages.

Genesis 18:22. Numbers 11:15. 12:12. 1 Samuel 3:13. 2 Samuel 12:14. 16:12. 1 Kings 12:16. 21:10. 21:13. 2 Chronicles 10:16. Job 1:5. 1:11. 2:5. 2:9. 7:20. Psalm 10:3. 106:20. Ecclesiastes 3:21. Jeremiah 2:11. Lamentations 3:20. Ezekiel 8:17. Hosea 4:7. Habakkuk 1:12. Zechariah 2:8 (12). Malachi 1:13. 3:9[117]

The Masora

---

[117] Appendix 33 from the Companion Bible:
http://www.therain.org/appendixes/app33.html

The Masoretes are early Jewish scholars, the successors to the Sopherim, in the centuries following Christ, who produced what came to be known as the Masoretic text. The Masoretes was well aware of the alterations made by the earlier Sopherim. Rather than simply remove the alterations, they chose to note them in the margins or at the end of the text. These marginal notes came to be known as the Masora. The Masora listed the 15 extraordinary points of the Sopherim, namely, 15 words or phrases in the Hebrew text that had been marked by dots or strokes. A number of these extraordinary points have no effect on the English translation or the interpretation. However, others do and are of importance. The Sopherim had a superstitious fear of pronouncing the divine name of God, Jehovah (Yahweh). Therefore, they altered it to read Adonai (Lord) at 134 places and to read *Elohim* (God) in some cases. The Masora lists these changes. The Sopherim or early scribes are also guilty of making 18 emendations, what they thought were helpful corrections, according to a note in the Masora. It appears that there were even more. It seems that these emendations were not done with bad intentions, as the Sopherim simply felt the text at these places were showing irreverence or disrespect for God or his human representatives.

Genesis 18:3 Updated American Standard Version (UASV)

³ and said, "Jehovah,[a] if I have found favor in your eyes do not pass by your servant.

[a] This is the first of 134 places where the Jewish Sopherim changed JHVH to Adonai. This replacement was made out of misplaced veneration of God's name.

Genesis 16:5 Updated American Standard Version (UASV)

⁵ And Sarai said to Abram, "May the wrong done me be upon you. I gave my maid into your bosom, but when she saw that she had conceived, I was despised in her eyes. May Jehovah judge between you and me." [a]

[a] "And you!" in the Masoretic text, is marked with extraordinary points by the Sopherim (scribes) to show that the reading "and you" is uncertain and should read, "and her."

Genesis 18:22 Updated American Standard Version (UASV)

²² And the men turned from there, and went toward Sodom: but Abraham stood before Jehovah.[a]

[a] This is the first of the Eighteen Emendations of the Sopherim, the only one in Genesis. An ancient Hebrew scribal tradition reads "but Jehovah remained standing before Abraham." Masoretic text, "but as for Abraham, he was still standing before Jehovah." The Sopherim might see have perceived this as Jehovah standing before Abraham, as showing irreverence or disrespect for God because it would appear to put Jehovah in a subservient position. Our Creator, sovereign of the universe, does not need to deliver a message to humans here on earth. In the Old Testament, we find many occasions where He has sent an angelic messenger in his stead.

The Consonantal Text

The Hebrew alphabet consists of 23 consonants, with no vowels. Unlike English though, Hebrew was not written from left to right but right to left. In the beginning, the reader had to supply the vowel sounds from his knowledge of the language. This would be like our abbreviations within the English language, such as "ltd" for limited. The Hebrew originally consisted of words made up only of consonants. Hence, "consonantal text" means the Hebrew text without any vowel markings. The consonantal text of the Hebrew manuscripts come to be fixed in form between the first and second centuries C.E., even though manuscripts with variants within the text continued to be produced for some time. Changes were no longer made, unlike the previous period of the Sopherim. *The International Standard Bible Encyclopedia* writes,

Text and Canon Prior to the discovery of the DSS [Dead Sea Scrolls], witnesses to the OT text and canon were principally the following: (1) the so-called Masoretic Text of the Hebrew Bible, which could more accurately be designated the received consonantal text and the text with vocalization and other pointing by the Masorites (MT)— they should not be confused, for the consonantal text is several centuries older than the MT; and (2) translations, such as the Septuagint (LXX) and Jerome's Vulgate. Other witnesses of significance included the Old Latin, the Syriac, the Samaritan, and other versions. The oldest extant Hebrew text was no earlier than the 10th cent[ury] A.D., but the versions give evidence that goes back to the 5th cent[ury] A.D. (the time of Jerome's work) and to the 2nd or 3rd cent[ury] B.C. (the time of the LXX). With the discovery of the DSS there is primary evidence, not merely that of translations, that goes back to 1stthe and 2nd (and possibly even the 3rd) cent[uries], B.C.

The text of the biblical MSS from Qumrân may be divided into two main categories. In one group are those portions that agree within reasonable limits with the consonantal text. (Since the DSS texts are not vocalized, they cannot be compared with the MT.) By "reasonable limits" is intended the inclusion of orthographic differences (such as *hw'h* for *hw'*, *lw'* for *l'*, etc.) that do not present any significant difference in the text. The second category includes those readings that clearly are not in agreement with the consonantal text. This second group could be further subdivided into readings that agree with LXX but differ from the consonantal text, and those that differ from both. Published studies indicate that certain OT books, such as Genesis, Deuteronomy, and Isaiah, are textually much closer to the consonantal text that others, such as Exodus and Samuel. The evidence leads to the conclusion that there were in existence in the first cents B.C. and A.D. at least three Hebrew text-types: the received text that formed the basis of the consonantal, the text that was used for the Greek translation, and a text that differs from both of these.

This conclusion should cause no surprise, for it was already indicated by at least two lines of evidence. The witness of NT quotations of OT passages indicates that some quotations can be traced to the Hebrew Bible (received text), some to the Greek version, and some to neither of these (the third text). It has sometimes been the practice to consider this third group of NT quotations as "loose dealing" with the OT text, but it is open to question whether a writer seeking scriptural authority for his statement would be allowed to handle the biblical passages with such abandon. The second line of evidence comes from Jewish tradition, where the formation of the "received text," often but questionably traced to the Council of Jamnia (sometime after A.D. 90), is described as taking the reading of two witnesses against one (*Taanith* iv. 2; *Sopherim* vi. 4; *Siphre* 356), in other words, working from three texts or text recensions that were in existence at the time.[118]

---

[118] W. S. LaSor, "Dead Sea Scrolls," ed. Geoffrey W. Bromiley, *The International Standard Bible Encyclopedia, Revised* (Wm. B. Eerdmans, 1979–1988), 893.

The Masoretic Text

Between the 6th and 10th centuries C.E., the Masoretes setup vowel point, and accent mark system. This would help the reader to pronounce the vowel sounds properly, meaning that there would be a standard, and no need to have the pronunciation handed down by oral tradition. Because the Masoretes saw the text as sacred, they made no changes to the text itself but chose to record notes within the margins of the text. Unlike the Sopherim before them, they did not take any textual liberties. Moreover, they drew attention to any textual issues, correcting them within the margins.

The devotement of the vocalizing and accent marking of the Masoretic text throughout this period was done by three different schools, that is, the Babylonian, Palestinian, and Tiberian. The Hebrew text that we now possess in the printed Hebrew Bibles is known as the Masoretic Text, which came from the Tiberian school. The Masoretes of Tiberias, a city on the western shore of the Sea of Galilee, established this method.

Unlike the Tiberian school, which placed their vowel signs below the consonants, the Palestinian school positioned the vowel signs above the consonants. Only an insignificant number of such manuscripts came down to us from the Palestinian school, showing that this system of vocalization was flawed. The Babylonian method of vowel pointing was likewise placed above the consonants. A manuscript possessing the Babylonian pointing is the Petersburg Codex of the Prophets, of 916 C.E., preserved in the Leningrad Public Library, U.S.S.R. This codex contains the books of Isaiah, Jeremiah, Ezekiel, as well as the "minor" prophets, with marginal notes. Textual scholars have readily studied this manuscript and compared it with the Tiberian text. While it uses the system of vocalization that places the vowels above the text, it follows the Tiberian text as regards the consonantal text and its vowels and Masora. The British Museum has a copy of the Babylonian text of the Pentateuch, which is substantially in agreement with the Tiberian text.

The Dead Sea Scrolls

In the spring of 1947, a Bedouin shepherd threw a stone into a cave, marking an event that would be heard around the world, making the name "Dead Sea Scrolls" more known than any other associated with archaeology. As he released one of his rocks into the cave, the sound of a breaking earthenware jar came back at him. Upon further examination, he discovered the first of the Dead Sea Scrolls.

The discovery of the scrolls rise to fame has been partly fueled by the controversy among scholars and the media. Sadly, this has left a public scandal, where those, not in the know, are thrown back and forth by confusion and misinformation. Stories have spread about an enormous conspiracy, driven by anxiety that the scrolls disclose details that would damage the faith of Christians and Jews as well. Nevertheless, what is the real importance of these scrolls? More than 63 years have now gone by; is it possible that the facts can be known?

The Dead Sea Scrolls: What are They?

The Dead Sea Scrolls are manuscripts of the Old Testament. Many of them are in Hebrew, with some being in Aramaic and a small number in Greek. Many of these scrolls and fragments date to the third and second Century B.C.E., almost 300 years before the birth of Jesus Christ. There were seven lengthy manuscripts in various stages of deterioration that had been acquired from the Bedouin.

Soon other caves were being searched, with new discoveries of scrolls and fragments in the thousands. A total of eleven caves near Qumran, by the Dead Sea, were discovered between 1947 and 1956.

Since, it has been determined that there are 800 manuscripts, once all the scrolls and fragment are considered. About 200 manuscripts, or about twenty-five percent, are copies of portions of the Old Testament. The other seventy-five percent, or 600 manuscripts, belong to ancient non-Biblical Jewish writings, divided between Apocrypha[119] and Pseudepigrapha.[120]

Various scrolls that produced the greatest interest for the scholars were formerly unknown texts. Among these were the interpretations on matters of the Jewish law, detailed instructions for the community of the Qumran sect, eschatological works that disclose interpretations about the outcome of Bible prophecy and the end times, as well as liturgical poems and prayers. Among them too were unique Bible commentaries, the oldest examples of verse-by-verse[121] commentary on Biblical passages.

---

[119] "The Protestant designation for the fourteen or fifteen books of doubtful authenticity and authority that are not found in the Hebrew Old Testament but are in manuscripts of the LXX; most of these books were declared canonical by the Roman Catholic church at the Council of Trent in 1546, and they call these books deuterocanonical (second canon)."—Geisler 1986, 637.

[120] "A word meaning "false writings" and used to designate those spurious and unauthentic books of the late centuries B.C. and early centuries A.D. These books contain religious folklore and have never been considered canonical by the Christian church."—Geisler 1986, 642.

[121] Of course, there were no verses in the ancient texts, as they were simply running text. It was Rabbi Isaac Nathan, while working on a concordance, numbered the Bible into verses in 1440 C.E. Robert Estienne (Stephanus) introduced his system for dividing the Bible's text into numbered verses in 1550 C.E., which we still use today.

The Dead Sea Scrolls: Who Wrote Them?

After carefully dating these fragile documents, it has been determined that they were copied or composed sometime between the third century B.C.E and the first century C.E. A handful of scholars have suggested that these scrolls were hidden in the caves by Jews that fled just before the destruction of Jerusalem in 70 C.E. However, the vast majority of scholars find this to be mere speculation, because the content of the scrolls tells something quite different. For example, many scrolls reveal an outlook and customs that were in conflict with the religious leaders in Jerusalem. The Dead Sea Scrolls disclose a community that held the belief that God did not approve of the priests and temple service in Jerusalem. On the other hand, they believed that God saw their form of worship in the desert as a substitute temple service until the return of the Messiah. Therefore, it is highly unlikely that the authorities at Jerusalem's temple would be in possession of such scrolls.

The Qumran community likely had a scriptorium (a room in a monastery for storing, copying, illustrating, or reading manuscripts); it is probable that people who became a part of the community brought scrolls in with them when they joined. Therefore, the Dead Sea Scrolls are a broad library collection. As applies to any extensive collection of books, the subject matter will be a wide range of thought, which will not reflect the thinking or religious worldview of any given reader within the community. Nevertheless, those texts, which encompass numerous copies, are more likely to take into account the general beliefs of the Qumran community as a whole.

The Qumran Residents: Were they Essenes?

Now that we have determined that, the Dead Sea Scrolls were the library of Qumran community, who were its people? Early on, in 1947 Professor Eleazar Sukenik obtained three scrolls from the Hebrew University of Jerusalem; after that, suggesting that these scrolls had belonged to The Essene Community.

First-century writers Josephus, Philo of Alexandria, and Pliny, the elder, are our primary source of information for this Jewish sect, the Essenes. There is no real consensus on their origin, but most scholars agree that they seem to have arisen following the Jewish Maccabean revolt in the second century B.C.E. The first-century Jewish historian Josephus described their existence during that period as he sketched their religious views as opposed to the Pharisees and Sadducees. On the other hand, Pliny talks about the whereabouts of a community of Essenes by the Dead Sea between Jericho and En-gedi.

Professor James VanderKam, a Dead Sea Scroll scholar, suggests, "The Essenes who lived at Qumran were just a small part of the larger Essene movement,"[122] which Josephus numbered to about four thousand. While this certainly does not perfectly fit the picture, what comes from the Qumran texts appears to match the Essenes better than any other known Jewish group in that period.

While dismissed by most scholars, a few have suggested that Christianity grew up out of the Qumran community. However, the differences between these two communities are far too great, even to take seriously such suggestions. For example, the Qumran writing contains an ultra-strict Sabbath regulations and an almost fanatical obsession with ceremonial purity. (Matthew 15:1-20; Luke 6:1-11) This would hold true as well with the Essenes' isolation from society, their position on the immortality of the soul, the stress they place on celibacy and spiritual concepts about sharing with angels in their worship. All of

---

[122] James VanderKam, The Dead Sea Scrolls Today. (Grand Rapids, MI: Wm B. Eerdmans Publishing, 2010), 127.

this puts them at odds with Jesus and the early Christian congregation.–Matthew 5:14-16; John 11:23, 24; Colossians 2:18; 1 Timothy 4:1-3.

No Conspiracy, No Secret Scrolls

Contrary to the cover-up theorists, after the Dead Sea Scrolls were discovered, numerous publications were released over the years that made those first finds accessible to scholars around the world. Nevertheless, the thousands of fragments from Cave 4 were proving far more awkward. These were not getting beyond the hands of a small international group of scholars operating in East Jerusalem (then part of Jordan) at the Palestine Archaeological Museum. The Jewish and Israeli scholars were strangely missing from this team.

Fueling this cover-up theory, the team established a rule of not permitting access to the scrolls up until they published the official results of their research. The number of scholars on the group was reserved to a fixed maximum. At the time of a group member's death, only one scholar would be added in his place. The volume of work required a considerably larger team, and in some cases, more expertise was badly needed in ancient Hebrew and Aramaic. James VanderKam worded it this way: "Tens of thousands of fragments were more than eight experts, however skilled, could handle."[123]

East Jerusalem and its scrolls came under Israeli jurisdiction after the Six-Day war in 1967. However, this did not result in a different policy change. This delay in publishing the scrolls of cave 4 went from years to decades; scholars around the world were in an uproar. Professor Geza Vermes of Oxford University, in 1977, called it the

---

[123] Ibid., 232

academic scandal par excellence of the 20th century. Stories were now spreading that the Catholic Church was deliberately concealing information that would shatter the long-held beliefs of Christianity.

The team of scholars was expanded to twenty in the 1980s. Then, in the 1990s, Emmanuel Tov, the newly appointed chief of the Hebrew University of Jerusalem, was able to get the number of scholars to fifty. At this point, they set a strict schedule for publishing the remaining scrolls.

However, in 1991, the development everyone had been waiting for arrived suddenly. First, *A Preliminary Edition of the Unpublished Dead Sea Scrolls* was published. This was put together with the assistance of a computer program, which reconstructed Cave 4 texts from a decades-old concordance. After that, the Huntington Library in San Marino, California, announced that they would make available to any scholars their whole set of photographs of the scrolls. After a short time, with the publication of *A Facsimile Edition of the Dead Sea Scrolls*, photographs of the formerly unpublished scrolls became available with no trouble.

Therefore, for the last two decades, *all* the Dead Sea Scrolls have been accessible for investigation. The examination discloses that there was no conspiracy; no secret scrolls that would have affected Christianity. Nevertheless, what significance does this investigation have for the average Bible student?

Why Should the Dead Sea Scrolls be of Interest Us?

Prior to the discovery of the Dead Sea Scrolls, the oldest manuscripts of the Old Testament were dated to about the ninth and tenth centuries C.E., known as the Masoretic texts (MT).[124] The Hebrew Old Testament was complete in the middle of the fifth century B.C.E., over 1,400 years earlier than these MT. Therefore, the question begs to be asked, 'can we trust this MT as really being the Word of God?' A member of the international team of editors of the Dead Sea Scrolls, Professor Julio Trebolle Barrera, states: "The *Isaiah Scroll* [from Qumran] provides irrefutable proof that the transmission of the biblical text through a period of more than one thousand years by the hands of Jewish copyists has been extremely faithful and careful." (F. Garcia Martinez, Martinez and Barrera 1995, p. 99)

The Isaiah scrolls identified as "lQisa^a" and "lQIsa^b" are complete copies of the book of Isaiah, but the latter is the earliest known copy of a complete Bible book. Both are from cave 1. Gleason Archer had this to say about the two Isaiah scrolls that "proved to be word for word identical with the standard Hebrew Bible in more than 95% of the text. The 5% of variation consisted chiefly of obvious slips of the pen and variations in spelling." (Archer, A Survey of Old Testament Introduction 1994, p. 19) Up to now, over 200 Biblical manuscripts have come out of the Qumran caves; representing portions of every Old Testament book except Esther. The Isaiah scrolls of Cave 1 are an exception to the rule, as most of the others are mere fragments, containing less than 10% of any given

---

[124] **Hebrew Bible:** the traditional text of the Hebrew Bible, revised and annotated by Jewish scholars between the 6th and 10th centuries C.E.

book. The books that are the most often quoted in the New Testament are, in fact, the most popular among the Qumran community: Psalms (36 copies), Deuteronomy (29 copies), and Isaiah (21 copies).

Aside from establishing that the Hebrew Old Testament has not undergone some radical changes over the last 1,400 years, the Dead Sea Scrolls also reveal two other important pieces to some long-standing questions. They provide evidence that there were different versions of the Hebrew Bible texts used by the Jews in the Second Temple period (537 B.C.E to 70 C.E.), each one of them containing its own variations. Of the scrolls, not all are identical in spelling and wording to the MT. Some of them are more in line with the Greek *Septuagint*,[125] also known by the Roman numerals for seventy, LXX.[126] It had been thought by scholars prior to 1947 that the differences in the LXX were the result of errors on the part of the scribes, even possibly intentional alterations by the translators. When the Dead Sea Scrolls became known, it was revealed that these differences were due to the variations of the different Hebrew versions. Further, this could possibly explain why writers from the New Testament quote from the Hebrew Bible texts using wording different than the MT.—Exodus 1:5; Acts 7:14.

Hence, the storehouse of thousands of fragments and Biblical scrolls affords the textual scholar an excellent basis in their studying the transmission of the Hebrew Bible text. Additionally, the Dead Sea Scrolls have established the

---

[125] **Greek version of Hebrew Bible:** a Greek translation of the Hebrew Bible made between 280 and 150 B.C.E. to meet the needs of Greek-speaking Jews outside Palestine.

[126] Because of the tradition about 72 translators, this Greek Bible translation came to be known as the *Septuagint,* based on a Latin word meaning "Seventy."

worth of both the *Septuagint* and the Samaritan Pentateuch for textual comparison. As all modern Bible are based on the Masoretic Text, they also provide added bases for these translation committees to consider emending (correcting) their translations and the MT.

It has long been held that there was not just one form of Judaism in the first century C.E. The portion of the Dead Sea Scrolls that describe the rules and beliefs of the Qumran community further validate that position. The Pharisees and Sadducees were far different from the Qumran sect.[127] Some extreme differences are likely, what led the sect to withdrawal into the wilderness. They saw themselves as the fulfillment of Isaiah 40:3,

Isaiah 40:3 Updated American Standard Version (UASV)

³ A voice of one calling out,
In the wilderness, "prepare the way of Jehovah;
  make straight in the desert a highway for our God.

Numerous scroll fragments state that the Messiah's coming was imminent. Bible student should find this interesting as Luke commented that "the people were in expectation, and all were questioning in their hearts concerning John, whether he might be the Christ [Messiah]."–Luke 3:15, ESV.

The Dead Sea Scrolls also help us better understand the historical setting in the life and times of Jesus Christ. They are also beneficial in the comparative study of Bible texts and ancient Hebrew. Nevertheless, not all of the Dead Sea Scrolls have been analyzed. Therefore, more

---

[127] Actually, there were more forms of Judaism. There were the Herodians, who were Jewish partisans or party followers of the Herodian dynasty. In addition, there were the Zealots, who advocated a Jewish kingdom completely independent of Roman control.

light may come out of the wilderness. Absolutely, these scrolls were one of the greatest archaeological discoveries of the 20th century, which remains to motivate both scholars and Bible students as we have now entered into the 21st century.

When Did the Hebrew Language Begin to Fade In Use?

Hebrew is the language in which the thirty-nine inspired books of the Old Testament were penned, apart from the Aramaic sections in Ezra 4:8–6:18; 7:12–26; Dan. 2:4b–7:28; Jer. 10:11, as well as a few other words and phrases from Aramaic and other languages. The language is not called "Hebrew" in the Old Testament. At Isaiah 19:18 it is spoken of as "the language [Literally "lip"] of Canaan." The language that became known as "Hebrew" is first shown in the introduction to Ecclesiasticus, an Apocrypha[128] book. Moses, being raised in the household of Pharaoh, would have been given the wisdom of Egypt, as well as the Hebrew language of his ancestors. This would have made him the perfect person to look through any ancient Hebrew documents that may have been handed down to him, giving him the foundation for the book of Genesis.

Later, in the days of the Jewish kings, Hebrew came to be known as "Judean" (UASV) that is to say, the language of Judah (Neh. 13:24; Isa. 36:11; 2 Ki. 18:26, 28). As we enter the period of Jesus, the Jewish people spoke an expanded form of Hebrew, which would become Rabbinic Hebrew. Nevertheless, in the Greek New Testament, the language is referred to as the "Hebrew" language, not the Aramaic. (John 5:2; 19:13, 17; Acts 22:2; Rev. 9:11) Therefore, for more than 2,000 years, Biblical Hebrew served God's chosen people, as a means of communication.

---

[128] The Old Testament Apocrypha are unauthentic writings: writings or reports that are not regarded as authentic.

However, once God chose to use a new spiritual Israel, made up of Jew and Gentile, there would be a difficulty within the line of communication as not all would be able to understand the Hebrew language. It became evident, 300 years before the rise of Christianity; there was a need for the Hebrew Scriptures to be translated into the Greek language of the day, because of the Jewish diaspora who lived in Egypt. Down to our day, all or portions of the Bible have been translated into about 2,287 languages.

Even the Bible itself expresses the need for translating it into all languages. Paul, quoting Deuteronomy 32:43, says, "Rejoice, O Gentiles ["people of the nations"], with his people." And again, 'Praise the Lord, all you Gentiles, and let all the peoples extol him.'" (Rom 15:10) Moreover, all Christians are given what is known as the Great Commission, to "go therefore and make disciples of all nations." (Matt 28:19-20) In addition, Jesus stated, "this gospel of the kingdom will be proclaimed throughout the whole world as a testimony to all nations." (Matt 24:14) All of the above could never take place without translating the original language into the languages of the nations. What is more, ancient translations of the Bible that are extant (still in existence) in manuscript form have likewise aided in confirming the high degree of textual faithfulness of the Hebrew manuscripts.

Many Hebrew Old Testament scholars hold the belief that the Jews switched from Hebrew over to Aramaic while they were exiled in Babylon for 70-years. However, there is no real strong evidence to support such a claim. History has shown us that groups of people who have been defeated, crushed, and enslaved for much longer than seventy-years have retained their native tongue. We must keep in mind, the Jews were well aware of the prophecies that one day God would intervene and return them to their homeland. It, therefore, stands to reason that they would **not** be moved to set aside Hebrew in favor of either Akkadian (Assyro-Babylonian) or Aramaic, the common languages of the day. Some will point to the fact that Aramaic passages and words are found in the exilic and postexilic books of Daniel, Ezra, and Esther. However, we must keep in mind that Daniel, Ezra, and Esther include records of events that took place in Aramaic-speaking lands, as well as formal communication, and they deal with the Israelite people who had been made subjects of foreign powers, who used Aramaic as a diplomatic language.

Nehemiah 8:8 Updated American Standard Version (UASV)

[8] They continued reading aloud from the book, from the Law of the God, **explaining it** and **putting meaning into it**, so that they could **understand** the reading.

Many have used Nehemiah 8:8 to say that the returned exiles could not perfectly understand Hebrew, so there was some Aramaic paraphrasing being done. While that might have been the case, what Nehemiah meant concerning this text is the exposition of the sense and how the Law was to be applied. (Compare Matt. 13:14, 51, 52; Lu 24:27; Ac 8:30-31) Look as you may, there is not one Scripture in all of the Bible that says the Jewish people abandoned their language, Hebrew, at any time as the tongue of their people. Yes, it is true, Nehemiah said, "In those days I also saw Jews who had married women from Ashdod, Ammon, and Moab. Half of their children spoke the language of Ashdod or the language of one of the other peoples but **could not speak Hebrew**." (Neh. 13:23-27) However, looking at the context of the indignation of Nehemiah at the Jews, who were involved in these pagan marriages with non-Israelites means that such slighting of Hebrew was very much disapproved. we would expect such when we think of the value they placed on the reading of the Word of God, which was primarily in Hebrew at this time.

From the close of the Hebrew Old Testament (Ezra and Malachi) from mid-fifth century BC (450) down until the penning of the book of Matthew, about 50 A.D., the Hebrew language is not mentioned in Scripture, for there are no canonical Old Testament books for this period. We have very few secular records as well. Of those scant few that we have, there is no major support for a move from Hebrew to Aramaic as far as the Jewish people are concerned. What we have are many of the Apocryphal books, such as Judith, Ecclesiasticus, Baruch, and First Maccabees, all being written in Hebrew, and these works are generally dated to the last three centuries before the arrival of Jesus Christ. Some of the non-Biblical writings found among the Dead Sea Scrolls were also written in Hebrew. In addition, Hebrew was used when the Jewish Mishnah was compiled after the death, resurrection, and ascension of Jesus Christ. The Mishnah was compiled **around 200** A.D. by Judah the Prince. Dr. William Chomsky says of the Mishnaic Hebrew: "This language bears all the earmarks of a typical vernacular employed by peasants, merchants and artisans. . . . On the basis of the available evidence, it seems fair to conclude that the Jews were generally conversant, during the period of the Second Commonwealth, especially its latter part, with both languages [Hebrew and Aramaic]. Sometimes they used one, sometimes another."—Hebrew: The Eternal Language, 1969, pp. 207, 210.

The substantial evidence supporting the belief that Hebrew continued on as a living language from the exile of Bababyin in 537 BC into the first century AD is found in the Bible itself where it refers to the Hebrew language in the Greek New Testament. (John 5:2; 19:13, 17, 20;

20:16; Rev. 9:11; 16:16) It is true that many scholars argue that the term "Hebrew" in these verses should instead read "Aramaic," yet there are very good reasons to believe that the term actually was a reference to the Hebrew language.

Another support suggesting that there was the use of a form of Hebrew in Palestine during Jesus' life and ministry here on earth, is early proof that the apostle Matthew first wrote his Gospel account in Hebrew. Papias of the first and second centuries wrote, "Matthew put together the oracles [of the Lord] in the Hebrew language." (*The Ante-Nicene Fathers,* Vol. I, p. 155) Early in the third century, Origen, in discussing the Gospels, is quoted by Eusebius as saying that the "first was written ... according to Matthew, ... who published it for those who from Judaism came to believe, composed as it was in the Hebrew language." (The Ecclesiastical History, VI, XXV, 3–6) Quoted in the same work are the words of Eusebius of the third and fourth centuries who states: "The evangelist Matthew delivered his Gospel in the Hebrew tongue." Jerome of the fourth and fifth centuries who said in his *Catalogue of Ecclesiastical Writers* that Matthew "composed a Gospel of Christ in Judaea in the Hebrew language and characters, for the benefit of those of the circumcision who had believed. . . . Furthermore, the Hebrew itself is preserved to this day in the library at Caesarea which the Martyr Pamphilus so diligently collected." (Translation from the Latin text edited by E. C. Richardson and published in the series "Texte und Untersuchungen zur Geschichte der altchristlichen Literatur," Leipzig, 1896, Vol. 14: 8–9.) Bible scholar, Hugh G. Schonfield's comments should also interest us. He writes on page 11 of *An Old Hebrew Text of St. Matthew's Gospel:* "As far back as the fourth century we hear of a Hebrew Matthew preserved in the Jewish archives at Tiberias." (Schonfield, Hugh. An Old Hebrew Text of St. Matthew's Gospel: Translated and with an Introduction

Notes and Appendices (p. 20). The Hugh & Helene Schonfield World Service Trust.)

G. Ernest Wright says, "Roman soldiers and officials might be heard conversing in Latin, while orthodox Jews may well have spoken a late variety of Hebrew with one another, a language that we know to have been neither classical Hebrew nor Aramaic, despite its similarities to both." *Biblical Archaeology* (Westminster Press, 1962, p. 243) Also, in *Daily Life in Bible Times,* Albert Edward Bailey offers the reader a picture of how Jewish youths were trained in the time of James, son of Zebedee:

> "Boys were trained in piety from their earliest days. This would mean that the boys had a knowledge of the Law, which they showed by being able to read it, write it and explain its obvious meaning. . . . The boys sat on the ground in a half-circle facing the teacher. There James was taught to read the Law in Hebrew beginning with the Book of Leviticus, the contents of which it was necessary for every Jew to know if he was to regulate his life acceptably to God; and he must pronounce the words correctly and reverently. Hebrew was a strange language to him, for at home and at play they spoke Aramaic, and later when he began to do business he would have to speak Greek. Hebrew was only for the synagogue. . . . After learning to read came writing, probably in Hebrew and certainly in Aramaic."—Pp. 248, 249.

Initially, the primary focus of the first seven years of Christianity was to bring in fellow Jews; thereafter, the Gentile population became more the target audience.

Therefore, we see that Matthew's publishing of his Gospel in two languages was simply responding to two audience needs. Therefore, Jesus Christ as a man on earth very well could have used a form of Hebrew and a dialect of Aramaic.

BIBLIOGRAPHY

Archer, Gleason L. *A Survey of Old Testament Introduction.* Chicago: Moody, 1974.

_____. *Encyclopedia of Bible Difficulties.* Grand Rapids: Zondervan, 1982.

Bercot, David W. *A Dictionary of Early Christian Beliefs.* Peabody: Hendrickson, 1998.

Bock, Darrell L. *Studying the Historical Jesus: A Guide to Sources and Methods.* Grand Rapids, MI: Baker, 2002.

Davis, John J. *Paradise to Prison: Studies in Genesis.* Salem: Sheffield, 1975.

Driver, G. R. *Canaanite Myths and Legends.* New York: T. & T. Clark, 1971.

Elwell, Walter A. *Baker Encyclopedia of the Bible.* Grand Rapids: Baker Book House, 1988.

Elwes, R. H. M. *A Theologico-political Treatise, and a Political Treatise.* New York, NY: Cosimo Classics , 2005.

Enns, Paul P. *The Moody Handbook of Theology.* Chicago: Moody Press, 1997.

Erman, Adolf, and H. M. Tirard. *Life in Ancient Egypt.* Whitefish: Kessinger, 2003.

Evans, Craig A. *Fabricating Jesus: How Modern Scholars Distort the Gospels.* Downers Grove, IL: InterVaristy Press, 2002.

Flemings, Hal. *Examining Criticisms of the Bible.* Indiana: Author House, 2008.

Friedman, Richard Elliot. *Who Wrote The Bible.* San Francisco: Harper Collins, 1997.

Garrett, Don. *The Cambridge Companion to Spinoza.* Cambridge: Cambridge University Press, 1996.

Garrett, Duane. *Rethinking Genesis: The Sources and Authorship of the First Book of the Pentateuch.* Grand Rapids: Baker Books, 1991.

Geisler, Norman L. *Inerrancy.* Grand Rapids, MI: Zondervan, 1980.

Geisler, Norman L, and William E. Nix. *A General Introduction to the Bible. Rev. and Expanded.* Chicago, IL: Moody Press, c.1986, 1996.

Habermas, Gary R. *The Case for the Resurrection of Jesus.* Grand Rapids, MI: Kregel, 2004.

_____. *The Historical Jesus: Ancient Evidence for the Life of Christ.* Joplin, MO: College Press, 1996.

Halley, Henry. *Halley's Bible Handbook.* Grand Rapids: Zondervan, 1988.

Hayes, John H., and Carl R. Holladay. *Biblical Exegesis: A Beginner's Handbook.* Lousiville, KY: Westminister John Knox Press, 2007.

Hoerth, Alfred. *Archaeology and the Old Testament.* Grand Rapids: Baker, 1998.

Hume, David. *An Enquiry Concerning Human Understanding.* Boston, MA: Digireads.com, 2006.

Jamieson, Robert, A. R. Fausset, and David Brown. *A Commentary, Critical and Explanatory, On the Old and New Testaments.* Oak Harbor: Scranton & Company, 1997.

Jay, Nancy. *Throughout Your Generations Forever: Sacrifice, Religion, and Paternity.* Chicago: University of Chicago Press, 1994.

Jones, Timothy Paul. *Misquoting Truth: A Guide to the Fallacies of Bart Ehrman's Misquoting Jesus.* Downers Grove: InterVarsity Press, 2007.

Kass, Leon R. *The Beginning of Wisdom: Reading Genesis.* New York: Free Press, 2003.

Keil, Carl Friedric, and Franz Delitzsch. *Commentary on the Old Testament.* Peabody, MA: Hendrickson, 2002.

Kitchen, K. A. *On the Reliability of the Old Testament.* Grand Rapids: Eerdmans, 2003.

———. *Ancient Orient and Old Testament.* Downers Grove, IL: InterVarsity Press, 1975.

Laux, John. *Introduction to the Bible.* Chicago: Tan Books & Pub., 1992.

Longman, Tremper III, and Raymond B. Dillard. *An Introduction to the Old Testament.* Grand Rapids: Zondervan, 2006.

McKenzie, Stephen L., and Stephen R. Hayes. *To Each Its Own Meaning: An Introduction to Biblical Criticism and Their Application.* Louisville: John Knox Press, 1999.

Morris, Henry M. *The Genesis Record: A Scientific and Devotional Commentary on the Book of the Beginnings.* Grand Rapids: Baker Books, 1976, 2007.

Murray, Hiebert D. *100 Reasons to Trust Old Testament History.* Galdstone: Westborne Study Center, 2005.

Nicholson, Ernest. *The Pentateuch in the Twentieth Century: The Legacy of Julius Wellhausen.* New York: Oxford University Press, 1998.

Price, Randall. *Searching for the Original Bible.* Eugene: Harvest House, 2007.

Pritchard, James B. *Ancient Near Eastern Texts,* 2nd ed. Princeton, NJ: Princeton University Press, 1955.

Rendtorff, R. "The Problem of the Process of Transmission in the Pentateuch." *JSOT,* 1990: 101.

Rooker, Mark F. *Leviticus: The New American Commentary.* Nashville: Broadman & Holman, 2001.

Speiser, E. A. *Genesis: Anchor Bible 1.* Garden City: Doubleday, 1964.

Spinoza, Benedict de. *Tractatus Theologico-Politicus* (Gephardt Edition 1925). Leiden: Brill Academic, 1997.

Stuart, Douglas K. *The New American Commentary: An Exegetical Theological Exposition of Holy Scripture: EXODUS.* Nashville: Broadman & Holman, 2006.

Wood, D. R. W. *New Bible Dictionary* (Vol. 1). Downers Grove: InterVarsity Press, 1996.

www.ingramcontent.com/pod-product-compliance
Lightning Source LLC
Chambersburg PA
CBHW060157050426
42446CB00013B/2878